# KEY GRIP

# Key Grip

A MEMOIR OF

ENDLESS

CONSEQUENCES

Dustin Beall Smith

*A Mariner Original*
Houghton Mifflin Company
BOSTON · NEW YORK · 2008

For information about permission to reproduce
selections from this book, write to
Permissions, Houghton Mifflin Company,
215 Park Avenue South, New York, New York 10003.

www.houghtonmifflinbooks.com

*Library of Congress Cataloging-in-Publication Data*
Smith, Dustin Beall, date.
Key grip : a memoir of endless consequences
/ Dustin Beall Smith.
p. cm.
ISBN 978-0-547-05369-1
1. Smith, Dustin Beall, date. 2. Grips (Persons) — United
States — Biography. 3. Authors — United States — Biography.
4. Motion picture industry — United States. I. Title.
TR849.S53.A3 2008
778.5'3092 — dc22 [B]      2008001530

Book design by Melissa Lotfy

Printed in the United States of America

EB-L 10 9 8 7 6 5 4 3 2 1

The author would like to thank the following publications in
which many of these essays first appeared: "No Feeling of Falling," *Alaska Quarterly Review;* "Starting at the Bottom Again,"
*River Teeth;* "The Second Person," *Hotel Amerika;* "Meeting at
the Water's Edge," *Louisville Review;* "Leaving the Garden" (originally titled "Working with the Savages") and "One Day," *Gettysburg Review;* "Just Pears" (originally titled "Still Life"), "The
Pipe," and "Grace," *Quarto;* "Augury" (originally titled "A Promise of Renewal"), *New York Times Magazine.*

*For my incomparable daughter,*
*Trellan Karr Smith*

# Contents

# *Augury*

---

BY MY SIXTEENTH YEAR as a key grip in the film industry, the glamour I once associated with making movies had long since disappeared. The grinding fourteen-hour days, the relentless pressure of budgets and scheduling, the dirt and grime in the studios, the incessant rhythm of building up and tearing down — all those things had so encrusted the Oscar, so to speak, that when it came to movie stars and all that hoopla, I couldn't have cared less.

But when I was called in September 1986 to interview for a film starring Jack Nicholson, all my professional cynicism crumbled, and I caught myself thinking as much about the star of the film as the technical challenge. When I watched a Nicholson film, I saw aspects of myself — in the womanizing Robert Dupea of *Five Easy Pieces*, the rebellious Randle McMurphy in *One Flew over the Cuckoo's Nest*, and the blocked writer from *The Shining*, Jack Torrance. I'd danced the proverbial edge. And I thought it would be fun to work with this guy who so perfectly captured the precarious pleasures of being a man in the modern world. I wanted the job — badly.

So I took off a couple of hours from the film we were shooting in Queens, and I showed up for my 10 A.M. interview at the Park Lane Hotel on Central Park South. The director of photography, a young Brazilian fellow, met me in the lobby. If, after our talk, he found me suitable for the job, he would then call the producers down from their suite to meet me. That was the drill. It was important to him that he make a sound decision since the person he chose as key grip would be responsible, along with the grip crew, for much of the lighting, many of the moving shots, and all of the special rigging — in other words, the behind-the-scenes, get-your-hands-dirty aspect of movie making.

We ordered coffee, and he told me I had come highly recommended by several people he knew. Then we talked. He told me about the script, which had been adapted from the William Kennedy novel *Ironweed*.

"Meryl Streep will costar," he said.

"Very cool," I answered.

We got along well, and I liked him, but he was holding something back. So I fell silent for a moment and stared at my coffee.

Finally, he said, "Do you mind if I ask you a personal question?"

"Of course not," I said. I knew what was coming.

"Do you drink?"

Just hearing the question was like being punched in the stomach. "Not for about five years," I said.

"But you used to? You had a problem?"

I was stunned. Why was my past being thrown on the table after all this time, and by a Brazilian who had just entered the country?

"Yes, I did. I had a problem," I said.

"I'm sorry to have to ask you such a thing," he said, "but the people upstairs brought it up. You are not on their list of candidates, it seems."

I could hear the door slam, but I didn't flinch. I thought of pleading that I was hardly the only person in the film business who had fallen victim to its once-fashionable excesses. But I didn't.

"All I can tell you," I answered, "is that I don't drink anymore."

"Fine," he said. "I want them to meet you."

Either he was being kind, I thought, or very naive. In any case, he asked me to wait. I sat there watching the rain fall in windy sheets over Central Park, and I knew I wasn't going to get the job.

Five years earlier, as a way of maintaining the edge that I had so blithely started walking in the 1960s, I was consuming *daily* several six-packs of beer, a fifth of Jack Daniel's, assorted wines and brandies, as much cocaine as I could get, and periodic tokes of marijuana to keep the lid on.

That was the summit of my consumption, and I teetered there for some time — until age forty-one, to be exact. The last time I tried to work on that regimen, however, I was fired. The ax fell in Philadelphia, during happy hour, when I climbed up on the bar, brandished the master key to the safe-deposit boxes of the hotel in which we were staying, and urged those present to help me loot the place. One of those at the bar happened to be Dino De Laurentiis, the executive producer of the film we were doing. They let me sleep it off, but the ticket home was under my pillow.

Two weeks after that incident, on Christmas Eve 1981, I quit. First the booze, later the cigarettes, and then the drugs — all the drugs.

With help, I started to pick up the pieces. Ripping the cover off the previous ten years, I found lying there broken friendships, busted love affairs, moldy dreams, unkept promises, a pathetic record as my daughter's father, an empty wallet, some IRS bills, and a directory filled with the phone numbers of people who would never hire me again.

No magic bullet could expunge this record. But somehow, time passed and life went on. People forgave or forgot or, increasingly, never even knew. I became stronger, the grade got easier, and soon I was chugging along like everyone else. I never had the urge to drink again. I rarely thought about the old days. They had become like an unexploded bomb buried safely in a field somewhere. Yet here I was, five years later, sitting in the dining room of the Park Lane Hotel, clutching the burning fuse.

This was the real price of my past life: there would always be an asterisk beside my name, a *maybe,* a whispered aside in the producer's office. Always. And I knew there was no way in hell a young director of photography, who knew this film was his big break, could possibly take a chance on me.

As it turned out, another man got the job — on his own merits, I'm sure. And I don't really know that my wild past had anything to do with the final decision. But the interview forced me to consider that it might have. I went back through my life and stood at old crossroads, reading signposts I might have followed, listening to warnings I could have heeded, and pondering choices that, if made differently, might have led to some more successful version of myself. The more I dug into my past, the more compelling my particular life became, failure or no failure. Events and forces mingled inextricably, overlapped and carried through like patterns on a weather map, until finally it seemed that it couldn't have been any other way.

For the first time in years, I felt a magical intent to my life. I remembered a day in March 1974 when my madness was more fun than it later became. I had climbed the Castle Pyramid in Chichén Itzá, Mexico, wearing a headband and beads and worn-out jeans. I stood on the highest step, a clear wind-blown ledge that looked out toward the Temple of the Warriors. It was late afternoon and there was no one around. So I sat down in my newly learned lotus position, straightened my back, and began to meditate. I uttered my mantra, felt the warm breeze push against my body, and went blank for a while. When I opened my eyes, I looked around and saw a small snakeskin rolling toward me from the shadows, a fragile, translucent promise of renewal.

# KEY GRIP

All the proofs that we are obliged to present, one after the other, of capacity for renewal, of resurrection or reawakening of being, must be taken as a coalescence of reveries.

— GASTON BACHELARD,
*The Poetics of Space*


For where the beginning is, there shall be the end.

— The Gospel of Saint Thomas

# 1

# Starting at the Bottom Again

---

I N 1996, AS I NEARED the end of my time in the film business, I began to notice an unusual preponderance of twenty-somethings running around movie sets, barking "Quiet!" and "Rolling!" and "Freeze!" the way prison guards yell at convicts during a lockdown. As they positioned themselves for a scramble up what they obviously had been taught was some kind of industry pyramid, I could detect nothing in their expressions that admitted to ignorance or suggested curiosity. This made me, at age fifty-six, with experience to share and things to teach, feel invisible.

I was ready for something new.

One day, on the set of a movie called *Cop Land*, I encountered a fellow whom I will call here "Arturo Has No Past." Arturo's features and skin color suggested he might be Filipino; he wore his shiny black hair in two shoulder-length braids. He worked as a loader in the camera department. I had noticed him scurrying on and off the set, lugging lens cases, and delivering fresh film magazines as needed. He was a union member in his midthirties, but he behaved like an intern — moving too fast in tight spaces and garnering more attention with his overly earnest behavior than his position on the pyramid warranted.

I first spoke to Arturo outside the sheriff's office set, where we had spent the whole of that August morning filming a heated scene between Robert De Niro and Sylvester Stallone. I was feeling a little deranged, having been caged for six hours in a ten-by-ten-foot office with two megastars who were consciously cultivating their rhinoceros-like personas. The stars' combined coterie of makeup artists, hairdressers, wardrobe specialists, bodyguards, and sycophantic studio executives had been sucking up most of the available oxygen. I had been fantasizing about shotgunning Sly Stallone and simply running out the door into some new future. The last thing I wanted to see, when I stepped outside for a bottle of water, was Arturo sitting on the plastic ice chest, chatting up a pretty extra.

"Get up," I said, jerking my thumb at him. Arturo leapt to his feet, opened the cooler, and grabbed an Evian. He uncapped it and offered me the bottle.

"*Hoka hey*," he said.

Having recently read about the famous Sioux warrior Crazy Horse, I recognized this to be a Native American greeting.

"*Hoka hey*," I said to Arturo, raising the bottle of Evian in salutation.

It is perhaps proof of my hunger for something new that I stood there in the shade, contentedly drinking water with pigtailed Arturo, whom I figured I had misjudged and now took to be a Lakota Indian (which would explain, I thought, his undisguised earnestness, if not his Filipino features and his Italian first name). I listened while Arturo entertained the pretty extra with stories of skydiving. By his own account he had made about 150 free-fall jumps. After describing the exhilaration of a long free fall, he turned to me and suggested, somewhat patronizingly, that maybe *I* would like to try jumping. I told him that I had already made well over six hundred jumps back in the early 1960s, before going to college. "I used to teach the sport, back in the day," I said, winking at the pretty extra.

Arturo had pretended not to be impressed. But over the course of a few days, my skydiving credentials kept us talking and eventually gave me an opening to pump him for information about his people.

On days when I gave Arturo a ride from our New Jersey location back into the city, where we both lived, I would bug him to tell me about Lakota rituals and life on the reservation. Arturo's answers, always slightly mysterious and tinged with an inexplicable reticence, intrigued the hell out of me. He was not entirely forthcoming about his Native identity, as if somehow the information he held so close to his chest was meant only for privileged ears. I was a sucker for such innuendo — anything to relieve the stifling boredom of a movie set. But I also had a genuine curiosity about the Lakota people, and I soon learned that Arturo's father was a medicine man on the Pine Ridge Reservation in South Dakota, and his grandmother was a medicine woman.

I began to see an opening into a new world, but I did not yet know what kind of opening and what kind of new world.

One evening, as we approached the inbound tollbooths on the George Washington Bridge, Arturo showed me the still-raw-looking scars on his pectoral muscles, where his pierced flesh had ripped as he broke free from the tree of life during a ceremonial sun dance presided over by his father. He talked of completing a prayer ritual called *hanblecheya*, which translates as "crying for a dream" and is popularly known as a vision quest. The ritual, he explained, involved being taken "up the hill" by his medicine man father and being made to sit alone on a blanket in the wilderness for four days and nights, without food or water. I had read about that practice in *Black Elk Speaks,* by John G. Neihardt, years ago. But that was back in the mid-1970s, when I was dabbling in spiritual things like pyramids, pendulums, crystals, and the writings of Carlos Castaneda and Emanuel Swedenborg. I had forgotten all about *hanblecheya,* but the ritual snapped back at me now with a new meaning. Suddenly it seemed quite compelling, even within reach.

"That's what I want to do," I told Arturo. "I want to go on a *hanblecheya.*"

"Then you will," he said.

"I want to meet your father," I said. "I want him to take me up the hill."

"That can be arranged," said Arturo.

"When?" I asked.

"When it's time." Arturo folded his arms across his chest and shut his eyes, managing to mimic the iconic stubbornness of a cigar-store Indian and avoid paying the bridge toll at the same time.

*Cop Land* wrapped in October. Although Arturo and I lived two blocks from each other in Manhattan and had figured out we even frequented the same corner restaurant on Broadway, I did not see or talk to him again for months. The new year came. I took work on a morose TV series called *New York Undercover.* During location filming in back alleys, jail cells, and dingy piano bars, I kept fantasizing about being led up the hill by Arturo's wise old medicine-man father. I envisioned him saying prayers over me and leaving me to sit on a blanket in a treeless area that looked like the high desert in California. I pictured visitations by coyotes, mountain lions, and snakes, and wondered if they would speak to me, as I had heard that animal spirits speak to seekers of wisdom. While it all seemed slightly ridiculous, I found myself returning to the imagined scene again and again, the way other people might daydream about a vacation at the golf course in Augusta. I felt drawn to it magnetically, as if I were putting myself in the way of a fast-approaching event that was meant to be.

By March, however, the fantasy had begun to fade from repeated exposure.

In early April, I ran into Arturo at the post office on 83rd Street. "*Hoka hey,*" I said. "When am I going up the hill?"

"Never ask me that again," he said. "*Never.* If it's meant to be, it will be." He made a sign with his right hand that seemed ridiculously imitative of the "How!" gesture in old Hollywood westerns. Then he turned and walked away. Even as a child I had found that gesture off-putting and wooden. I began to wonder about Arturo.

When the month of May went by without a word from him, I wrote him off as a charlatan and made tentative plans to take a July vacation in Mexico with Angie, my new live-in girlfriend who was twenty-three years my junior.

One Friday evening in late June, having dragged myself home after a killer week on *New York Undercover,* I checked my messages. There was only one: "*Hoka hey.* Get ready. We leave in four days. No sex, starting tomorrow."

After persuading Angie to postpone our vacation, I bought a three-hundred-dollar Pendleton blanket from Camps and Trails and began preparing my tobacco ties in the manner Arturo had prescribed over the phone. I was to string together seven hundred two-inch squares of folded broadcloth (seven colors in all), each square containing a few fingers full of tobacco. The resulting 150-foot string of ties was to be wrapped around a piece of cardboard, so it wouldn't tangle as it was being unwrapped when I was up the hill.

"Tangles," Arturo had warned, "portend catastrophe."

· · ·

On the drive to South Dakota, Arturo slept and meditated in the front seat of my 1987 Honda Accord. Miffed by my insistence that he wear a seat belt, he hardly spoke to me. Occasionally I would ask him questions.

"What if coyotes surround you when you're up the hill?"

"Pray."

"Do people ever die on *hanblecheya?*"

"Yes."

"What about lightning?"

"You'll see."

The first night we pulled into a rest stop in western Ohio. Arturo slept in the car; I slept on the ground under a tree. In the morning I discovered him walking backward around my Honda, holding a metal plate filled with burning prairie sage. Mumbling incantations, he wafted smoke at the tires. A small old-fashioned leather suitcase lay open on the hood of the car. Inside I could see what looked like medicine man paraphernalia, including a colorful ceremonial pipe. When Arturo finished smudging the Honda, I asked him why he had been walking backward around the car. In my reading about the Lakota I had learned of the *heyokas,* the so-called contraries, who conducted sun dance ceremonies in which they did everything backward. They were said to have visions and dreams of lightning and could immerse their hands in boiling water without harm. They were known to read minds and see right through people. Their ceremonial function was to expose social and spiritual hypocrisy and to poke fun at traditional ceremony. Even in everyday life *heyoka* medicine men were thought to be eerily powerful and, because of their unpredictable behavior, terrifying.

I could not have articulated, then, why I found it so unsettling to watch Arturo walking backward around my car, smudging it, and mumbling prayers. Perhaps it was the seemingly nonsensical combination of the bizarre and the intentional.

Watching him, I remembered many years earlier having seen a magician in Central Park, a young fellow dressed all in black and wearing white face makeup, who was performing in front of a sizable audience. In one continuous gesture he had rolled up both sleeves and produced out of thin air a full deck of cards. Those were my drinking and drug-taking days, when I was accustomed to altered states and felt capable of staring almost anything in the face. But when this magician turned his blank gaze toward me, I felt caught in his snare. He fanned open the deck of cards, closed it, and fanned it open again. Each time he repeated this gesture, the size of the deck got smaller, until eventually it seemed no larger than the wing of a moth. Suddenly he opened his hand, and the deck was gone. My whole body shuddered; the blood drained from my head.

Not that I was about to shudder or grow faint in front of Arturo. But I did ask, trying to conceal my anxiety, "You're not *heyoka*, are you, Arturo?" He didn't answer me. I asked if his father lugged medicine around in a bag like that.

"He doesn't have to. People come to *him*," said Arturo.

"How old is your dad?" I asked.

"Forty-three," said Arturo.

I did the calculations. "He had you when he was eight?"

Arturo said nothing. Annoyed, I stopped asking questions.

The second night, we stopped at a rundown motel near the Nebraska border. In the morning, I sat outside my room and composed a letter to my daughter, Trellan, using a portable Smith Corona typewriter. It felt oddly comforting to pound away on the same machine I had used when she was a baby, as if by doing so I could restore the relatively short-lived sense of family that had existed at the time. I told her where I was and where I was going, and then I wrote "I love you" and signed it "Dad."

I also practiced pronouncing the Lakota words *mitakuye oya-*

*sin,* which I had been told would be essential to utter when entering the sweat lodge. Arturo had warned me the night before that if I was to go up the hill the following day, we must rise with the sun and arrive at his father's place "six hands before sunset."

He emerged from his motel room, perfumed and pigtailed, at ten o'clock in the morning.

We drove to a Wal-Mart, where we bought four cans of Bugler tobacco, six cartons of Marlboros, ten shopping bags filled with food, four gallons of milk, boxes and boxes of Kool-Aid, gifts for the family — one for each of Arturo's seven brothers and sisters, ranging in age from three to twenty — and a twenty-four-inch chain saw for his father, to help prepare for the sun dance. Arturo perused the western-style shirts while I paid for everything with my credit card. He arrived back at the car just in time to watch me lash the last of the stuff to the roof rack.

"First thing you do," Arturo said, jumping in the front seat, "is give my father the chain saw. Then, the next chance you get, offer him a fistful of tobacco, with your hand turned down like this. If he takes it, tell him you want to go up the hill."

"And if he doesn't?" I asked.

"Then you'll have to turn around and drive home. Alone. Got it?"

"Got it," I said.

The option of turning around and heading home was beginning to appeal to me. I missed Angie. I had met her and asked her to move in with me during the nearly yearlong hiatus that followed my first contact with Arturo. And my relationship with her had begun to represent the new start I had been seeking after *Cop Land.* It would have taken little effort on my part to decide that this trip to visit Arturo's father was nothing but an errant and risky detour. That I didn't suggests I may have had less choice in the matter than I thought.

• • •

The speed limit in South Dakota is seventy-five miles per hour. I kept the needle at ninety. Hot air whipped at the open windows, pulsed in my eardrums. My left elbow cooked in the sun. My pen burst, bleeding black ink onto the dashboard. The oppressive heat, the broken air conditioner, the monotonous highway — it all seemed to conspire with Arturo's moody silence. Every time I glanced at him his eyes were closed. I envied him, really.

We had traveled entirely on interstates through Pennsylvania, Ohio, Indiana, Illinois, Iowa, and seen the same American inanity all the way. The topography had long since given way to the replica world — replica restaurants, replica gas stations, replica malls. I had hitchhiked through here in the mid-1950s, before the interstate system existed, when each state differed radically in character from the next. No boundaries anymore, or so it seemed.

Arturo sat up and looked around. "Turn here," he said, pointing to an exit sign.

"Where are we?" I asked.

"*Turn here,*" he demanded.

I cut close in front of a tandem semi and hit the exit ramp at seventy. We came to a halt at an intersection off U.S. 83. It was two o'clock. It felt good to be off the highway, but I realized with some dismay that I wasn't quite ready to leave the tedious security of the interstate. I felt relieved to see a McDonald's a few hundred yards to the right. I could call home from there, check my messages one last time before entering Indian country, grab a predictable meal. I had eaten nothing since early morning.

A mockingbird landed on a section of busted snow fence. Arturo studied the bird and thanked it for giving him directions. Then he pointed to the left.

"We're late," he said.

"I'm hungry," I said. But I turned left anyway and headed south, away from the replica world.

•  •  •

The Lakota Sioux live on seven large reservations, located mainly in South Dakota. Arturo and I had planned to take I-90 all the way west to Rapid City and cut south through the Badlands into the Pine Ridge Reservation. This sudden change of plan, which now took us through the Rosebud Reservation, was oddly unnerving. I hadn't said any final goodbyes. I had packed a cell phone deep in my luggage, but it didn't feel appropriate using such technology on a trip whose theme was essentially spiritual. What if something happened to me out here? Who would ever know how far I had gotten or what my state of mind had been? What would the crew and cast of the film I was scheduled to work on in August make of my disappearance?

Huge thunderheads gathered in the west. The gently undulating terrain on either side of the two-lane highway gave off an electric glow in the filtered sunlight. Things did grow here — prairie grass and sage — but they grew tenuously. An inexplicable dread began to take hold of me. This wavelike landscape felt claustrophobic compared to the flat route described by the interstate. I could no longer make out where we were headed or see beyond the next rise. I wanted wings and visibility.

The highway had no guardrails, even where the land fell away from the road. Aside from some dilapidated cattle fencing, the only hint of civilization was the occasional diamond-shaped road sign that asked, WHY DIE? Arturo explained to me that one of the preferred methods of suicide on the reservations was to get shit-faced and head-on another car.

"Oh, good," I said.

Arturo laughed. "No seat belts on the rez," he said, unbuckling his. He took out his Nikon and snapped my picture. I shot him back with my Olympus, which I kept handy in the glove compartment. Apparently energized by this spontaneous interaction, he donned his headband and a pair of goggle-like shades, then slithered out the passenger-side window to sit on the window ledge, his legs the only part of him still in the car. I slowed down, but he hollered at me to go faster.

"Okay, asshole," I yelled.

The needle hit seventy, and I held it there as we crested the next knoll and dipped into a shallow valley. I imagined him hanging on to the roof rack, defying the wind. It reminded me of the times I had ridden the wings of biplanes when I was a skydiver — hanging on for dear life, my jump suit whipping in the wind, my heart pounding. The sheer exhilaration of it came back to me in a rush of memories.

Arturo started to crawl out onto the hood, camera in hand. Holding on to one of the wipers, he lay down on his right side and shot some weird angles of me through the windshield. I returned the favor, half expecting to see him blow off the hood like a leaf or butterfly. Watching him out there, his cheeks buffeted by the wind, his pigtails flapping, his maniacal war-whooping self grinning at me, I began to buy into this foolishness and started swerving the car from one side of the road to the other. Twenty years ago it would have been me out there on the hood — drunk, perhaps — egging the driver on.

The clowning around didn't last long though. Now that I was older, I knew better. Macho behavior had long since ceased to produce enough adrenaline to sustain itself for very long.

I motioned for Arturo to get back inside. He crawled up over the windshield to the roof rack and stayed out of sight for a while. I held our speed. As I waited for him to slither back through the window, I realized that in a few hours I would be standing in front of his medicine-man father, who, if he really *was* forty-three, couldn't possibly be Arturo's father, but would be fourteen years my junior. At age fifty-seven, I would be begging the man's permission to participate in a ritual that was originally intended to turn boys into men.

· · ·

I questioned whether it was an eagle or a turkey buzzard, but when Arturo said that the bird soaring high above us was a good omen, I played along. I gave him the good old thumbs-up, punched in a tape of Eric Clapton's *Unplugged,* and turned up the volume on "Layla."

"Getting close?" I asked.

Apparently we were. Arturo was now communicating with any raptor in sight — and there were many, both in the air and perched on utility poles. I contented myself with reading the occasional road sign. We had left the Rosebud Reservation, driving west on U.S. 18, and had passed through prosperous farm country — white owned, probably. It wasn't lost on me that I breathed easier when I saw silos and farmhouses; all I had seen in Rosebud were cinder-block huts, rundown shanties, and rusted trailer homes.

"White farms," said Arturo.

The thunderheads in the west had vanished, easing my anxiety. I felt slightly wiggy from all the driving and anticipation, and I barely noticed when we entered the Pine Ridge Reservation.

The land looked fertile. An old Buick, filled with Indians, flew by us in the opposite direction. The driver waved.

"My father will probably ask you why you've come," said Arturo.

"You haven't told him about me?"

"Not about you. He expects me to arrive next week, for the sun dance."

"You mean we're just showing up here with no warning?"

"He'll ask you why you want to go up the hill. Be ready for that."

"Jesus fucking Christ, Arturo, you mean you haven't even *told* him about me?"

"That's for you to do."

I wanted to grab Arturo's braids and smash his head into the dashboard. *What a pitiful generation!* I thought. But I drove on into the sun, trying to think of a clever answer for his father. I figured I would need to say something with special import, or I would be sent packing. "I have come to your land to pray" might do, but I couldn't say such a thing with a straight face; I knew nothing about prayer. "I have journeyed here from afar, these many days, to find myself." Nope. "Life is long, but time is short . . . How, brother medicine man! . . . *Hoka hey!* I have come to your reservation to seek a vision!"

It was hopeless. Why *had* I come? Because the film business had proved to be an empty, soulless detour from what I considered my higher purpose? Yes. I remembered a dream I had had decades earlier, a puzzling dream in which I hit an exhilarating home run on some ancient playing field but failed to touch first base on my way home. A psychotherapist had suggested that the dream perfectly described my intuitive nature: I had no trouble reaching a conclusion, he said, but struggled constantly to know how I got there. Quick to see the ending of any given project, I rarely felt the need to finish it. For a writer, he cautioned, this spelled trouble. True, but how could I explain that to a medicine man? It was too long a story. And what could a medicine man know about writing anyway?

I decided to say, simply, "I've come here because I've always known I would." That had a certain ring of truth, and it seemed to shed a little light on the inexplicable nature of this trip — admitting to a degree of powerlessness on my part. Yet it also maintained a modicum of authority appropriate to a man of my age and experience. This answer had a certain dignity I could live with.

Arturo ejected my Eric Clapton tape, tuned in the local FM station, KILI, and turned up the volume. The speakers exploded with the high-pitched warble of powwow singers accompanied

by a thundering drum. A chilly spike of fear shot up my spine.
Arturo told me to turn north on BIA 27 rather than continue
into the town of Pine Ridge. I didn't protest, but I wanted to.
Perhaps it was just my hunger — I don't know — but the dread
had returned in full force. I suddenly felt completely powerless.
Or maybe "beyond help" is a better way to put it. Arturo had
made it clear we were now out of cell phone range. My presumably lofty decision to come here had quickly morphed into the
hard reality of actually being here. An approaching four-wheel-
drive police car slowed down to check us out. Two uniformed
Indians eyed us from behind their sunglasses as they passed.
No one lived along this road. The shrill music evoked visions
of the scalp-taking warriors in the western movies of my youth.
As a child I had always sided with the war-whooping Indians
who ambushed the cavalry. But westerns weren't about the Indians in those days. It was the life of the cavalryman you got to
know — the blue uniform and the gold scarf and the romance
and the danger of it all. And it was the seduction of belonging to
the winning side that won out in the end. Now, that treble war
whoop made the roots of my hair sting. I thought of the *heyoka*
again.

"Your dad's not *heyoka*, is he?" I asked, turning down the volume. Getting no answer, I assumed the answer was no.

"Tell me his name, at least," I said.

"Little Boy," said Arturo. "Mike Little Boy."

"But your last name is — "

"I earned that name," said Arturo, curtly. "It's a warrior's
name."

I had no idea what that meant but decided not to pursue the
subject for fear of encouraging Arturo's annoying grandiosity.
"Do I call your father Mike?" I asked.

"That's his name," said Arturo.

"You're a nasty fuck," I said.

Arturo laughed. We came to an intersection marked by a small sign that read WOUNDED KNEE.

"Pull over here," Arturo said. "I'm gonna pray."

I pulled off the road and negotiated a rutted car path that traversed an overgrown hillside, atop which sat Wounded Knee Cemetery. It looked pretty much like any overgrown graveyard, which, given its history, made the place particularly chilling.

Arturo grabbed a fistful of tobacco from the Bugler can between his legs. "Wait here," he said.

I got out of the car but kept a respectful distance while Arturo stepped inside a gated chainlink fence at the monument's perimeter. He held the tobacco up to the four directions, mumbling some Lakota words.

In this place, on December 29, 1890, approximately 250 Lakota men, women, and children were senselessly slaughtered by the U.S. Seventh Cavalry. I remembered reading the shocking fact that ten soldiers had been awarded the Congressional Medal of Honor for their cowardly deeds that day. The massacre coincided with the beginning of reservation life for the Lakota people. Black Elk, who had witnessed the aftermath, called it "the end of a beautiful dream."

From where I stood I could see hundreds of faded tobacco ties hanging from the low chainlink fence. I could make out some of the names etched on the south side of a small granite obelisk: Chief Big Foot, High Hawk, Ghost Horse, Wounded Hand, Scatters Them, He Crow . . .

I looked around. Down by the road a lone Indian was snoozing behind the counter of a makeshift arts-and-crafts concession, sound asleep in the shade of a cottonwood tree. I tried to imagine the massacre — the frozen ground, the bodies dismembered and ripped to shreds by Hotchkiss cannon fire — but I couldn't. In the stillness of the midsummer air I felt overwhelmed, not by the heightened resonance of this historic site, but by the full force of its anonymity. It could have been a modest cemetery anywhere in America. Its seeming lack of grandeur mirrored my own feelings of insignificance. Suddenly I missed New York City. I leaned against my Honda and took a leak.

Arturo returned to the car. "If I die on *hanblecheya,* that's where my father will bury me."

"And if *I* die on *hanblecheya?*" I asked.

"It depends," he said. "They'd probably just toss your body in a field, like a dog."

Mike Little Boy lived three miles east of the Porcupine Trading Post, a general store with a single gas pump that constitutes the entire commercial center of Porcupine, South Dakota. Porcupines have a way of warding off the curious, and the town appeared true to its name. The windows of the little store were boarded up to prevent theft. The young woman behind the counter seemed remarkably hostile. I paid for a tank of unleaded and looked around at the selection of edibles — potato chips, candy bars, canned Spam, ketchup. "Have a good day," I said to the girl. She responded with a sneer.

"She expected you to ask if you could use her father's phone," explained Arturo, when we stepped outside. "White people do that. They butter her up then bum the phone."

I shrugged and nodded. But I wasn't happy that we had landed in this place. The sun was now just over four hands above the horizon, which my wristwatch confirmed as half past five.

"Let's get there," I said. "I want to go up the hill tomorrow."

We drove east from the store until we came to a hand-lettered sign that read END OF THE ROAD. We turned left and bounced along a narrow, heavily rutted driveway, past some skinny palominos and two slapped-together houses. At a clump of cottonwoods the ruts deepened. I had to drive up a steep embankment, then accelerate downhill, gunning the poor Honda through a section of thick mud that would have challenged a tank.

Then suddenly we were there.

We stopped in front of a brown house with aluminum siding — one of those wide-load prefabs you see taking up too much of the highway on a flatbed semi. Just to the left of the house sat a pine cabin, Depression era, probably. Next to the newer house it looked sadly askew on its cinder-block footing. A brood of puppies appeared from beneath the cabin, their bodies wagging ambitiously toward us before they changed their minds and retreated into the shade.

"The whole family was raised in that cabin," said Arturo.

I killed the engine. What had I imagined? Not a tepee, but not this either. The front yard was strewn with junk that looked as if it had been lying there for years, half buried in the mud and overgrown with weeds. A ragged upholstered sofa and a single metal folding chair sat directly beneath the gutterless eaves, just to the left of the front door. Broken tricycles, bicycles, plastic toys, rusted chain saws, useless carburetors, plastic bottles, aluminum cans, dented tire rims, busted wrenches, scattered drill bits, a crosscut saw, old sweatpants caked with dirt, soiled Pampers, a Yankees cap stuffed into the spout of a dented five-gallon gas can, a beat-up Toro lawn mower missing a rear wheel. Between the house and cabin, more trash, and beyond that — to the west — a clothesline weighed down with bright laundry. Curtains hung limp in the windows of the house; the front door lacked a knob. A dust-covered Buick with a broken windshield sat baking in the sun.

"That's my dad's car," said Arturo. "Good old rez car." He told me to back my vehicle away from the house so his mother would have room to park her Pinto. I let the Honda roll back down the driveway until it stopped. We got out.

Arturo pointed toward a domed heap of sun-faded blankets surrounded by tall weeds. "That's the sweat lodge," he said. "You're gonna sweat tonight."

A dilapidated blue trailer sat on cinder blocks in a field across from the house. The sun dance grounds were partially visible on a knoll several hundred yards to the east. From where we stood they looked like a small-scale version of Stonehenge — a circular affair constructed of vertical pine poles and partially roofed with pine boughs.

The rest was wide-open plains, spreading out in all directions — undulating and resonant but, to my eye, not particularly hospitable.

Arturo started removing his personal stuff from the back seat. I began unlashing the carton containing the new chain saw, which had made the trip on the roof of my car. I had just freed it and hoisted it off the rack when I noticed someone walking toward us — a wiry guy, about five feet ten, wearing beat-up cowboy boots, oily jeans, and a greasy brown T-shirt with a cigarette pack rolled up in the sleeve. He sported dark glasses and a Chicago Bulls visor cap. A lit cigarette dangled from his mouth. What I could see of his face looked dark and leathery and deeply lined. He shuffled along the stony driveway like an old man who had just got out of bed. But he wasn't old. If I had seen him coming on a New York sidewalk, I'd have crossed to the other side of the street.

"Hey!" he said, still thirty feet away. The word issued from his mouth like a growl, and I felt sure we had stopped at the wrong house.

I tapped Arturo on the shoulder.

"That's my dad," he said.

Immediately, I set the carton back on the roof, ducked into the car, and grabbed the can of Bugler from the passenger's seat. I stuffed tobacco into my left pants pocket as fast as I could and stood up in time to see Arturo shaking hands with the man.

"What you come here for so early?" said his father.

"We're gonna help you get ready for the sun dance," Arturo said, taking a step back.

"I was *wondering* what those two red hawks meant," said his father. "I seen 'em earlier. You see 'em on your way in?"

Arturo seemed inordinately nervous and signaled for me to give his father the chain saw. Obediently I took the box off the roof again and held it out. Arturo's father stared at the Sears brand name, letting me hold the box out to him just a few seconds longer than necessary. For a split second I felt like one of the three Magi bringing an offering to the manger. It wasn't a comfortable sensation.

Finally he took the box and passed it to Arturo. "Put this in the house," he said, "and go tell Mike Junior to gas it up. We gotta go for wood. We're gonna sweat tonight."

And off ran Arturo, as eagerly as a little boy, in the same exaggerated way he went about his work on a movie set, ducking low as he ran, as if under fire. His father chuckled at the sight, the sound erupting from deep in his throat. Then he called to Arturo, "Hey, Dances With Wolves! Bring me and your friend here a soda pop too."

"Mister Little Boy?" I asked.

"Yep," he growled, working his lower jaw and pouting his lips. I realized he was toothless. "*Mike* Little Boy."

"I'm Dusty, from New York City." He held out his hand. As we shook, I dug into my left pocket, came up with a huge fistful of tobacco, and offered it to him, with my hand turned down. Again he hesitated just a touch too long, staring at me from behind his glasses, still holding my right hand in a loose grip.

When finally he accepted the tobacco, I blurted out, "I want to go up the hill, on *hanblecheya*."

He nodded, took off his sunglasses, and hung them from the neck of his T-shirt. I saw now that his eyes looked mean, maybe even cruel. No kind old medicine man, this guy.

"Why?" he said, putting the clump of tobacco on the car hood.

"Why *what?*" I asked. Suddenly I had forgotten how I was going to answer the all-important question.

"Why do you want to go up the hill?" he asked, gesturing that I should feel free to just spit it out, but looking at me with undisguised impatience, perhaps even contempt. My well-rehearsed, meaningful, urbane answer had deserted me entirely. This toothless, weather-beaten Indian — *this junk yard dog,* I thought — had completely unnerved me. Would he even be able to *understand* a sophisticated answer? Probably not. In any case he was waiting for a response of some kind. I could see by his no-nonsense expression that everything hinged on it. Yet I couldn't come up with a thing.

"I don't know," I said.

The sun bore relentlessly into my neck.

"How long you thinking of going on *hanblecheya?*" he asked.

"Four days and four nights," I said, trying to infuse my response with warriorlike resolve. But I didn't put enough breath behind the words, and my assertion lingered in the air like a pop fly. I felt completely weakened.

"One day," said Mike. "Maybe."

"What?" I said.

"I'll let you go up the hill for one day — maybe. We'll have to ask the spirits in the sweat lodge tonight."

"Hey," I said, pointing at my license plate, "I came a long way for this. I've got to go up for four days."

"Nope," he said.

"*What?*"

Arturo returned with two cold cans of Coke. I declined. Mike snapped open one of the cans. "Get a knife," he said to Arturo. "Go cut five chokecherry stakes for your friend here. He's going up tomorrow morning, coming down tomorrow night." Arturo went running off again before I could ask him to intervene for me.

I had told Angie that I would be going up the hill for four days and four nights. I had made it sound — hinting at the substantial physical risk and inflating the spiritual dimensions — if not exactly heroic, at least exotic. I had done the same with my daughter, my brother, my sister, and anyone else who would listen.

When I was in my thirties and living alone, I used to leave cryptic notes on my kitchen counter before taking any kind of road trip: a stanza of poetry, say, that would hint — in case I failed to return — that I had foreseen my death. Not a suicide note by any means, but a hedge against fate. Something that would allow my death to draw attention to my otherwise unremarkable life. It had always felt strange to return home, alive and unscathed, and then have to read those cryptic notes. I felt a similar letdown now. I would have to tell everyone that my *hanblecheya* had been like a picnic on a hill — that I had been turned down for the real ordeal.

"Listen, Mike," I said, "I come from New York City, but I've spent a lot of time in the wilderness by myself. I've spent *weeks* alone camping out. I can handle it."

"You don't understand," he said. "It's different here at my place. You see up there?" He pointed in the direction of a sparsely wooded hilltop, about half a mile to the north. I hadn't really noticed the hill before, which seemed odd now because it looked quite ominous from here, where the low angle of the sun highlighted some scraggly hilltop pines, accentuating their shadowed side.

"I see it," I said.

"That's a sacred hill," he said.

I stared at Mike. Nothing in this man's face indicated to me that he knew what *sacred* meant; in fact, he seemed all too acquainted with the profane. Clearly life had bitten him; you could read it in his eyes, and in the fight scars on his face. I had seen pictures of famous medicine men — Black Elk, Lame Deer, Fools Crow — and they were always old men with weathered faces and wise, sardonic eyes. They were men you could trust. *Sacred hill because you say so*, I thought. *Sacred because it's on your property.*

"It's different than what you read in books," said Mike. "A lotta guys can't even stay up that hill for two hours — even Indians. They start to see things. When you come to me, it's not like up in Bear Butte where they tell any white guy who comes along, 'Okay, do four days, take water with you, whatever you want, you wanna be Black Elk, we'll make you Black Elk.' That's not the way I do things."

"I can go four days," I said.

"Maybe," said Mike, nodding. "But what if you can't?"

It had never occurred to me that I couldn't, just that I might die trying. But I didn't want to tell him that. Suddenly it seemed pathetically naive that I hadn't even acknowledged the possibility that I might fail to go the distance.

"It's like this," said Mike. "Maybe I say, 'Okay, do four days and four nights,' and then in the middle of the first night you change your mind because some coyote comes up behind you and says, 'Yip!,' or the lightning gets real bad, or a rattlesnake wants to curl up and have sex with you, and then you come running down the hill, screaming, and bang on my door, waking up my wife and kids. 'What happened, Mister Little Boy! Help me! Help me!'" Mike was whining in falsetto now, and distorting his toothless mouth, like Popeye. "'What the hell happened to me up there? Why didn't you tell me that was going to happen?' You see? And then the word gets around and people start to talk about you because you said you were gonna do something, and you didn't do it. It's no good when people start talking about you like that. You see what I mean?"

I said I did. It was like when I was teaching skydiving and a student would go up in an airplane with me and then decide not to jump after all. I knew what Mike meant. I didn't want to be seen as some failed wannabe around here, or when I got home.

Then, as if he had read my mind, he said, "I don't mean people around here," he said, "or your friends back home. I mean the old ones, up there." He pointed to the hill. "The spirits know who you are."

"Spirits?" I said

"They come to you," said Mike. "You'll see."

I had always assumed that the notion of spirits — humans taking animal form, or animals taking human form — was meant metaphorically. But as I looked at Mike, I didn't see any evidence that he was using a figure of speech, or that he was even capable of such a thing. I backed off a little and signaled my acquiescence — and my disappointment — with a shrug. *Whatever*, I thought.

A slight breeze kicked up, bringing with it a rotten odor — garbage or rattlesnakes, I couldn't tell which. A naked child appeared on the front steps of the house, turned sideways to us, and peed into the dirt. I could see Arturo, down by a little creek, bent over and hacking away at a chokecherry sapling. The drone of a television set emanated from behind the front door; a police scanner crackled behind a curtained window.

I had driven eighteen hundred miles in just over two days. My body was still buzzing from the long drive, and already I wanted to head back.

I glanced at the so-called sacred hill and started to unlock the trunk of my car. "We brought some food," I said to Mike. *Two hundred fucking dollars' worth of food*, I thought.

Just then Mike touched my arm. His knuckles were black with grease, a mechanic's hand. I pulled my arm away.

"There's something you need to know," he said.

"Shoot," I said. I was still pissed off.

"When you come down from the hill tomorrow night, every-thing will be different for you."

*Yeah,* I thought, *I'll be on my way out of here.*

"You'll be changed," he said.

*Yeah, right,* I thought. I remembered a time when I was nine-teen. The actor Kirk Douglas flew into the airport in Orange, Massachusetts, where I taught skydiving. He had one of his young sons in tow. I ran up to him and excitedly tried to get him to make a parachute jump, telling him at great length what a kick skydiving was. He listened patiently and then said, "Are you telling *me* about *kicks,* kid?"

Was Mike really telling *me,* a sophisticated urban man who had been living a fast-paced, cutting-edge life in the film busi-ness, about *change?*

"The spirits are gonna come, and they're gonna want to talk to you," said Mike, "but you can't step off the blanket when they do. The tobacco ties are there to protect you. You just gotta hold your pipe and pray real hard."

"I don't have a pipe," I said.

"I'll give you one of mine. But you gotta hold on to it all the time you're up there."

This drivel was making me impatient. Was Mike really try-ing to convince me that spending a single day on a blanket was going to be a big spiritual deal? I toed the dirt with my sneaker, unearthed a small stone, kicked it away. When I looked up I saw that Mike's expression had softened, and I realized that all this while he had been speaking to me quite warmly, albeit with a warning tone. I recognized in his eyes the same concern I used to project while speaking to student jumpers just before they left the airplane, or to apprentice grips before they performed their first dolly shot on a film set. I urged the beginners to get the most out of the experience, but was careful to remind them of the difficulties and warn them of any inherent dangers. Sud-

denly I felt grateful that Arturo's father wasn't just rubber-stamp-
ing my request to go up the hill for four days and four nights
without food or water (a life-threatening proposition, at best),
grateful that he had cut me down to size. Stripped of my heroic
conceit, I thought, *Hey, I know what kind of guy this is. He's not
so bad. I see what he's doing. I've been this way with apprentices
myself. We stand on equal footing.* Thus deluded — blinded by the
illusion that I already knew what he had to teach me — I con-
ceded the role of teacher to him.

"Okay," I said, "tell me. How will I change?"

"When you come down from your *hanblecheya*," he said, "everything will seem strange. You won't know how to think about
it right away. You might even be scared. When you go back to
New York your life there won't make sense anymore. You'll go
back to work, and you'll think about us here when the sun goes
down, and you'll remember what happened to you when you
were here. You'll still have your family and your job and your
people, but it won't be the same. This will be your home." He indicated the surrounding plains.

"But that will still be my *real* home," I said, pointing east toward New York. The words tumbled out like those of a little boy
whose mother is dragging him away from his playmates.

The sun dipped below the roofline of the Little Boy house,
casting a shadow over us. Mike told me that unless the spirits
in the sweat lodge said otherwise, I would go up the hill for one
day this year, one day and one night next year, two days and one
night the third year, and two days and two nights the fourth, in
the year 2000.

"Four years?" I asked, unable to conceal my dismay.

But Mike had apparently told me all I needed to know for
now. Gone was the kindly expression on his face. Once again
I was looking at the hard-bitten mug of a man whom I never
would have picked out of a lineup as a medicine man.

That's when it hit me.

"Are you *heyoka*, Mike?" I asked.

"You bring any cigarettes?" he said.

I pointed at the car trunk, where I had packed the cartons of Marlboros.

"Good," he said, with a throaty chuckle. He jerked his thumb in the direction of his Buick. "I'll need some gas money too."

The front door of Mike's house opened into the living room, which was separated from the kitchen by a counter. I began lugging the gifts and groceries into the house, two bags at a time. Four young Lakota men sat on a sofa, watching TV, while a fifth sat on the edge of an old easy chair, swatting away the hand of the boy I had seen on the porch. The child, named Wambli (meaning "eagle"), was trying persistently to touch the new chain saw.

As I went back and forth between kitchen and car, I attempted to make eye contact with the young men, even saying hello once. But they avoided looking at me, preferring, it seemed, to scope out the contents of the shopping bags. On my third run, one of them stood up and grabbed a bunch of bananas from a bag and passed them to his friends. The fellow next to him began rubbing his thumb across the six-inch blade of his bowie knife. He stared at my midsection as if planning to gut me.

I made four or five more trips until all the grocery bags were heaped on the muddy kitchen floor. A half-eaten hamburger bun, pinned beneath the leg of a chair, reminded me that I had eaten nothing but a blueberry muffin all day. A peanut butter and jelly sandwich came to mind, but as I looked around, the idea faded. Flies worked every available kitchen surface. Dishes lay in the sink, stacked higher than the faucet. The stovetop was encrusted with ketchup, mustard, and burnt coffee. The refrigerator door, held ajar by a huge mound of frost, lacked a handle. Packaged meat, crammed into the freezer section, appeared gray and speckled. The refrigerator shelves overflowed with inedible leftovers. I left the kitchen and went back outside to put my car trunk in order and tidy up my personal belongings.

After about ten minutes I heard Mike call my name from the porch. I rolled up the car windows, took a deep breath, and reentered the house. Arturo and Mike were standing in the center of the living room. The sullen guy with the bowie knife stood up to give Mike a seat on the sofa, then he left the room, eyeing me coldly as he went out the door. Arturo put the five chokecherry stakes in a corner and started to unwrap a toy airplane for Wambli.

I didn't know what to do with myself. I wanted to be introduced, but all eyes were on Wambli, who now threw the balsa wood airplane against the wall, breaking its right wing in half. Everyone's attention drifted to the television, which featured a talk show with a bunch of white women gabbing about relationships. I gazed at the mostly bare walls, embarrassed. I felt ashamed of the television and the people on it, as if it and they and I had somehow conspired to create the plight of the people in the room. An old Pendleton star blanket hung on the wall opposite the sofa, serving as a backdrop for some curled three-by-five-inch family photographs, each held in place by a single thumbtack.

"You got them cigarettes?" said Mike.

I went to the kitchen, fished around in the bags, and came back with a carton of Marlboro Reds.

"Just one pack," said Mike. "Put the rest on the counter."

"May I use your bathroom?" I asked.

Mike jerked his thumb over his shoulder. It was a small house.

"Be right back," I said, though I wanted to crawl out a window and drive away to the Comfort Inn we'd passed several hundred miles ago. But instead I walked through the kitchen and down a short hallway, past three small bedrooms. Clothing was heaped everywhere. Judging by the garments on the floor, girls slept in the room closest to the kitchen. A rack of barbells, a slew of hand weights, and a poster of Madonna identified the boys' room. I assumed that Mike and his wife slept in the room where the police scanner continued to squawk, though nothing really distinguished the room as adult.

I closed the door to the tiny, windowless bathroom and flipped up the toilet seat. The whole thing crashed to the floor, lid and all, revealing a shit-speckled, piss-streaked porcelain bowl. The wet bath mat stank of mildew. Two muddy bath towels lay draped over a shower door that had slid off its track. Both the showerhead and the bathtub faucet leaked a steady stream of hot water. The sink spigot dripped cold. Over the sink four bent nails marked the space where a mirror had once hung. A banged-up hair dryer, plugged into an unprotected socket, dangled from an old shelf bracket.

I replaced the toilet seat, rinsed my hands, wiped them on my pants, and returned to the living room.

Everyone but Mike had left.

"Get out there and help Arturo," he said. "We're gonna sweat in a couple of hours."

I set up my orange tent on rough ground about fifty feet west of the sweat lodge. Arturo made camp in the little Depression-era cabin. As I drove the tent stakes into the hard earth, smoke drifted toward me from the fire pit located in front of the sweat lodge. Arturo and I had piled fifty-four rocks, per Mike's instructions, atop a tower of dry pine logs. The crackle and snap of the fire made me feel as if everything was going to be okay. I secured the fly over my tent, tossed my inflatable mattress and sleeping bag inside, zipped the door shut, and walked over to the sweat lodge.

Shaped like an upside-down bowl, about twelve feet in diameter and four feet high at its apex, the lodge was constructed of tied-together saplings covered with layers of old blankets and tarps, which are meant to keep out light and hold in heat. With the door flap open, a dank, musty smell wafted from its dirt-floor interior.

A raised, earthen altar in front of the sweat lodge consisted of a circle of small rocks with a weathered buffalo skull in the center. Next to the skull Arturo had placed Mike's medicine pipe and a large rattle decorated with feathers. Having grown up in a family in which religion took a back seat to art, I found most altars strange. This one had all the elements of child's play, but felt deeply spooky to me.

I changed into shorts and stood alone by the fire. The sun sat less than one hand above the horizon. The air was cooler now; the fire coals intense. The heated rocks — most of them about eight inches thick — glowed like volcanic magma beneath layers of gray ash. I still hadn't eaten but was neither hungry nor thirsty. For a few moments I indulged in a kind of reverie, taking in the wide expanse around me: the vast horizon, the seemingly endless pasture where skinny horses grazed beyond my tent. I let myself imagine living there. My tent would make a perfectly ample home. Compared to the parks in New York City, there was some real elbow room here. And a blessed silence, broken only by a whisper of wind.

Then the Indians came roaring in. Mike's Buick, loaded with the young men I had seen earlier, skidded to a halt five feet in front of me. Two more rez cars, filled with men, women, and children, pulled up next to my tent. Four children piled out of the lead car and ran directly over to my Honda. After glomming the contents of the change tray and glove compartment, they began playfully jumping on the hood and roof. I imagined having to hitchhike home.

Soon the sun touched the horizon and the mosquitoes came out. Everyone gathered around the fire. I said hi to the kids and nodded hello to two old women — the only people who seemed willing to acknowledge my presence. The men made no pretense of welcoming me, nor did the young woman who stood on the other side of the fire. But I didn't feel shy about looking at each of their faces, firelit and dark, their skin the color of bloodwort. For some reason it seemed okay to be staring at them — as if their reticence invited me to stare and thus become part of the group.

A tall string bean of a man, who looked to be about forty, stood at the edge of the fire pit next to his wife. He poked at the rocks with a pitchfork. Neither he nor his wife spoke a word.

Mike showed up, followed closely by Arturo, who was lugging a plastic five-gallon spackle bucket filled with water. Mike told me to help Arturo put the red-hot rocks into the sweat lodge, and as we began forking them into the rock pit, Mike wrapped a beach towel around his waist and removed his pants and shirt. His hairless chest was covered with raised scars that resembled exit wounds, evidence of many years of piercing during sun dances, the annual sacrificial ceremonies that the U.S. government had outlawed for much of the twentieth century.

When we finished forking the fifty-four rocks into the lodge pit, Mike said something in Lakota that made everyone laugh. When I looked around, I saw that everyone was amused by *me*. The string-bean man said something in response, and everyone roared again, even harder. Nervously I looked down at my feet, at my white Reeboks covered with ash. My fly was wide open. Mike explained, in English, that his brother-in-law, Lanford, wanted to know if I was planning to feed the mosquitoes a little dick. The kids doubled over with laughter as I zipped myself up. An old woman told me not to worry; it was just in fun. The young men shook their heads as if they had never in all their lives seen such a dumb *wasichu*.

People started preparing for the sweat — the women wrapping themselves in ragged sarongs, the men stripping off their shirts and putting on shorts. Every man present, except me, sported weltlike scars on his chest and back.

I hung my shirt and eyeglasses on a fence post and stood aside politely, as if waiting for the host to seat his guests. Mike, already seated inside the sweat lodge just to the right of the door flap, waved the women in first. I watched as the four of them crawled inside, moving clockwise around the hot stones until they sat to the right of Mike. I wanted to be the last one in so that I too could sit next to the door. But Mike told me to crawl in now — and to sit all the way in back.

"You get the seat of honor," he chuckled. "The *hot* seat."

I dropped to my knees and muttered "*Mitakuye oyasin*," as Arturo had trained me to do, then I crawled somewhat tremulously around to the back. *Mitakuye oyasin* translates variously as "all our relations" or "we are all related"; the *we* refers both to all races and to all beings, including the four-legged and winged, and of course the spirits. I sat cross-legged, directly opposite the door, fighting off the feeling that I was way too large for the space assigned me. How would I find my way out of here in the dark? The hot rocks blocked my path.

A fat spider crawled up my left calf and across my thigh. I folded my arms to avoid provoking it.

Arturo made his way past my knees and sat to my left. The other men entered and closed ranks at my right. Lanford sat down at the north side of the door, a round drum and leather-tipped drumstick on his lap. I was hemmed in now for the duration.

A fourth car pulled up outside. Its headlights went out, and I heard two doors slam. I watched through the door flap, incredulous, as more people undressed outside. I could see a bit of the black horizon and a triangle of indigo sky, pierced by a single bright star. I focused on that star and pinned all my hopes on it. *Don't let me panic.* The intense heat from the rocks was already cooking my knees. My eyeballs felt dangerously dry.

An overweight woman wearing shorts and a tank top crawled through the door and sat next to Mike. Three more men crawled past Lanford, forcing everyone even closer together. I was knee-to-knee now with Arturo — and with the sullen guy who had been fiddling with the bowie knife earlier.

"Watch the kids," Mike said to a teenage girl outside. "Don't let them be banging on that New York car."

Suddenly the door flap fell and it was dark. The guy on my right leaned closer and whispered in my ear, "Hey, Custer, this is your last day on earth."

I blinked, and then blinked again. I had never been in this kind of darkness. When the first ladle of water hit the rocks, my whole body stiffened. Sizzling drops splashed my kneecaps, and steam engulfed my face. I gasped and cupped my hands over my nose. Another splash, another surge of steam. I could tell by the spitting sound that buckets of water could be poured on those rocks before they would even begin to cool down.

I heard Mike say from the other side of the darkness, "We're gonna do four doors tonight, in honor of our friend here from New York."

I didn't know what "four doors" meant, but I was sure it wasn't pleasant.

Lanford started banging the drum, and Mike began to sing:

> *Wahkathaka usimala ye!*
> *Wanikta cha echamu yelo . . .*

Everyone took up the song with him. Another splash of water, and all the available oxygen was consumed by steam. My breath fled my lungs, as if sucked out by a tornado. I squirmed backward, my spine pressed against a ridgepole. I tried to topple sideways, get down where I could breathe. No room to move. I sat up straight, seeking air above. It was hopeless. I gasped.

The drum kept an insistent one-two, one-two rhythm, with the accent on the first beat. When I was a boy, I used to play an album of 78-rpm records called *The Little Indian Boy.* Whenever the boy was lost, his father would drum for him just like this. In the dark now, this childhood memory collided with thoughts about my own father, who had died sixteen months earlier, sparking an intense feeling of loss.

It seemed no one knew how to hold a tune. With Mike leading the way, everyone shouted the song. I started bellowing too, faking the words, rocking my upper body back and forth in time with the drum, and holding my hands over my face to shield my eyes from the steam. This song seemed to last forever. I imagined blisters bubbling on my face, my hair combusting spontaneously. Forget the dangers of *hanblecheya* — I was going to die right here.

When the singing stopped, Mike said something about my going up the hill the next morning, or at least I assumed that was what he said because I heard my name mixed in with Lakota, as well as the word *hanblecheya.* Everyone said, "*Aho!*" which I took to be supportive. Then Mike shouted, "*Mitakuye oyasin,*" and the door opened at last. Steam poured out into the night.

The star I had seen earlier had sunk below the horizon. The water ladle was passed around the lodge, starting with Lanford, and each participant took a sip. When it came to the fellow on my right, he took a drink, tossed the remaining water on the rocks, and passed the ladle back the other way.

"Anyone else want water?" asked Mike.

I kept silent for fear of seeming unmanly.

I glanced at Arturo. In the dim light of the coals I could see that his eyes were closed, his posture erect, his pigtails hanging on his chest. He looked every inch the warrior he claimed to be.

The ladle went the other way. The women drank, and the door was closed again. Again the steam surged, thicker and thicker. A new song began:

> *Thukasila Wakhathaka*
> *Eya hoyewaye lo . . .*

When I heard moans of agony coming from the guy on my right, I began rocking back and forth in earnest, gasping for air. "Oh, God," I intoned, "help me breathe." Other people were singing. I tried to join in but kept slipping into the begging mode. "I want to live!" I said into my cupped hands. "Let me live through this!" When the singing stopped, more water hit the rocks, and the place became even more unbearable. I was going to die in a dark sweat lodge as payment for the sins of my race. The guy with the bowie knife was right: I probably *was* General Custer in a former life. I did in fact have Indian-killer blood running through my veins, and I chose this very moment to remember the details. My seventh great-grandmother, nine generations back, had killed and scalped twelve Nipmucks in revenge for the killing of her newborn child. Hannah Emerson Dustin, my namesake. Her statue, with bloody scalps hanging from her victorious fist, still stood in Concord, New Hampshire — right there on Contoocook Island in the Merrimack River, where she had done the dirty deed back in 1697. This was karmic revenge.

"Forgive me," I mumbled into my hands.

I was about to yell this contrition out loud to the spirits when I realized that the singing had stopped and someone else was speaking, in English. I had no idea who — the voice issued from the vicinity of the drum. A man was saying he wished he hadn't gotten drunk the night before; he had said things he didn't mean and behaved badly. He prayed for his mother and his sisters. *"Aho!"* said the others. *"Aho!"* I said, happy to recognize a soul as miserable as me. Then another man spoke, and another, either in English or Lakota, and the circle of prayer revolved toward me.

The fellow on my right simply said *"Mitakuye oyasin"* and tapped my arm. I squeezed my eyes shut — as if it mattered — and started to speak, addressing Tunkasila (meaning "grandfather") first, as the others had done. I said nothing about being Custer, and I didn't ask forgiveness for my race or for my murderous ancestor. Instead I heard myself praying for the people on the reservation, for the Little Boy family, and for my family and friends back home. I ended with *"Mitakuye oyasin."* I couldn't recall ever having prayed in public before.

Arturo said, *"Mitakuye oyasin,"* thus passing the prayer to the old women, whose petitions took forever. I wanted to scream. Lanford beat the drum to give them a little privacy. When the door opened again, everyone collapsed as low as they could, trying to find breathable air. No one spoke.

During the third door Mike asked the spirits about me. He concluded that I was to go up the hill for one day — dawn to dusk. He told me that the spirit of Fools Crow, a famous medicine man who had died a few years earlier, would accompany me. As he spoke, little sparks blossomed in the pitch-black air, as if someone were flicking a Zippo lighter, although no sound accompanied the sparks. I heard a rattle being shaken. Then everyone sang again. It felt like Hades in there. The bowie knife guy to my right began to retch. My pores were bleeding sweat.

During the fourth door we joined in a nearly endless song of thanksgiving. It was the hottest door of all.

Dripping wet, we crawled out into the cool night air. At least an hour had passed, or maybe a lifetime. I staggered to my feet like a newborn calf. One of the men vomited into the fire pit; another fell onto an outstretched bath towel. The stars were out in force.

Mike lit his pipe and we stood in an informal circle, sharing a smoke. I felt completely drained and wanted to laugh. I thought of cold spring water and pictured the peanut butter and jelly sandwiches I was going to devour in the house.

"Got your tobacco ties together?" asked Mike.

"Yep," I said. "Blanket, tobacco ties, chokecherry stakes."

"Good," he said. "Arturo will give you one of my pipes tomorrow morning. He's gonna take you up the hill. Now go to your tent, and don't talk to anyone until you come down tomorrow night. No food, no water."

I stepped into my sneakers, hoping to at least say goodbye to the people with whom I had just suffered so intensely. But everyone, including Arturo, deliberately avoided looking at me — knowing, I suppose, what I was in for.

Everyone, that is, except the guy with the bowie knife. From him I got a nod.


The next morning, as I waited for Arturo to fetch me from my tent, I tried to imagine my *hanblecheya*. Arturo had given me the drill, more or less, during our drive west: I would be confined to an "altar" the size of my Pendleton blanket, which in turn would be surrounded by a perimeter of tobacco ties. Holding a long-stemmed pipe, I was supposed to pray until the sun went down, after which I would go through a second sweat ceremony and some kind of debriefing session, conducted by Mike. Even though I had gone without food or water for about twenty-four hours, I figured I could get through the *hanblecheya* well enough.

But what about obtaining a vision? Would I be able to cry for a dream? Or was I too self-conscious, too cynical? And what kind of dream or vision could I expect? Might I discover, at last, the true me, and be ready to take up where the old me had left off? What would it mean if I had no vision at all? I wasn't sure I wanted to know.

I unzipped my tent flap. A brown-and-white female mutt, the mother of the puppies I had seen on our arrival, sat outside slapping her tail in the dirt. Her swollen teats tugged at her loose skin, accentuating her rib cage. One eye had gone milky white, but with the other she eyed me affectionately. Another dog, part German shepherd, lay sprawled in the shade on the west side of the tent. This beast had kept me awake most of the night, nosing and pawing the nylon walls, sniffing at the mosquito netting, growling at my every move. He raised his head to look at me.

By the time Arturo finally showed up with my prayer pipe, the sun had risen two hands above the horizon. He looked both annoyed and guilty about being late. He put a finger to his lips, silencing me, and signed that he needed the key to my car. I had just pocketed the key in my sweatpants, which I planned to wear that day. The rest of my belongings were locked in the trunk and the glove compartment.

"You can't take any metal up the hill," said Arturo. "And leave your eyeglasses down here."

The idea of Arturo having access to my car, credit cards, cash, and eyeglasses was something I hadn't anticipated. How could I cry for a dream with that kind of worry on my mind? Bad enough that I wasn't allowed paper and pen. How could I see a spirit clearly without my glasses? But I turned them over to Arturo, along with the key, and sat in the passenger seat with my necessities on my lap: one large blanket, one small camping blanket, one pipe, five chokecherry stakes, and 150 feet of carefully wrapped tobacco ties. The car was already oppressively hot. I squinted at the dashboard clock: 8:20 A.M.

Arturo got in behind the wheel and said he would need some money for the feast his family planned to prepare when I got down from the hill that night. I took the key from the ignition, unlocked the glove compartment, and removed my wallet.

"Tell me when to stop," said Arturo, shutting his eyes and bunching his fingers like a monkey.

I opened my wallet and watched as he blindly extracted one bill at a time. I began to imagine scrambled eggs and bacon, pancakes and fresh strawberries, a mug of French roast coffee, a tall glass of chilled Evian water. I pictured feasting victoriously to the cheers and congratulations of admiring Indians. I didn't flip the wallet shut until he had removed five twenties.

Arturo tucked the money in his shirt pocket and opened his eyes. I tossed the wallet back in the glove compartment, locked it again, and handed back the key.

We drove away from my tent, passing an old chicken coop with a clothesline out front. Maneuvering between two wooden fence posts, we headed out across the rolling, trackless plains. Arturo didn't say a word. Tall grass and sage scraped the under-carriage of the car as we bounced for half a mile over prairie-dog mounds. Nearing our destination, I turned in my seat and saw the mutt bitch and the German shepherd following us in hot pursuit, their tongues dangling from their mouths.

I had pictured a normal hilltop, a place from which I would have a commanding view of the Great Plains — the better to in-spire a vision. But when we arrived at the edge of the sparsely wooded area, it became clear that the hilltop itself was actually concave, like the apex of a volcano. The sparse trees I had seen from Mike's house grew out of that declivity, disguising the hill's true shape.

Weighed down with paraphernalia, I followed Arturo and the two dogs, who had caught up with us, into the hollow. Scrawny, widely spaced pines struggled to keep a foothold on the slope.

We paused for a moment in front of one tree, the limbs of which were festooned with discarded tobacco ties — black, red, white, and yellow — some faded by the sun, some bright. Strands of spider silk stretched like guy wires between the smaller branches.

We continued down, weaving our way through fallen tree trunks and low brush. When we reached the bottom of the declivity, Arturo began pacing with the focused intensity of a dowser looking for water. But instead of using a dowsing rod, he held out his palm, apparently feeling the aura of the place. He searched the sky as if seeking avian guidance. Satisfied, he nodded and told me to spread out my blanket.

How could I ever see the sunset from the bottom of this bowl, this ungodly swale? No horizon, no majesty. I wouldn't have thought of stopping here to piss, much less settled here for *hanblecheya*. But I spread out my blanket.

"Take off your sandals," said Arturo. "Put them off the blanket, upside down."

I obeyed, quietly calculating the hours that remained — twelve, roughly. The ground Arturo had picked was lumpy and uninviting.

"Stand in the center and start to pray," he said. "Don't let go of that pipe, ever."

I picked up the pipe and cradled it in my arms, in rough imitation of a loin-clothed medicine man I had seen in an Edward S. Curtis photograph. I faked the praying, sneaking looks at Arturo, who drove the chokecherry stakes into the ground, one at each corner of the blanket. When he had sunk a fifth stake, to indicate west, he attached one end of my string of tobacco ties and began winding them from stake to stake, around and around, laying out the colors in reverse order of the way I had tied them in New York City. He walked backward, moving clockwise around me. The dogs watched.

Done with the ties, Arturo recited something in Lakota, slowly and with sincerity. Then he simply walked away, in the direction of the car. The bitch sniffed my sandals and plopped down next to them. The German shepherd leapt over the ties and joined me on the blanket. I clapped my hands loudly to get Arturo's attention and signal him to take the dogs back with him. I clapped again and again, but he ignored me. I tried to whistle, but all that came out was a hiss. By the time I called his name he was gone.

"Get out!" I ordered. "Go away!"

Unaccustomed to commands in English, the shepherd leapt playfully at my outstretched hand and got hold of my shirtsleeve with his teeth. The bitch tried to join us in what she took to be play, but instead of springing over the tobacco ties, she just barged through them. I yelled at the shepherd and punched him hard in the side, trying simultaneously to push the bitch away with my foot. She got the message and backed out, dragging down the north side of my altar. The shepherd, however, got serious and started fighting for the space.

"That's enough," I said. "Get out of here, leave me alone!"

The dog came at my left arm again, and again I nailed him with my right fist. His mood changed, his confidence mounting in direct proportion to my anger and frustration. He arose and came at me on two legs, his forepaws pushing at my chest. I grabbed his neck fur and tossed him sideways, but he recovered and bounded toward me again. There was nothing playful in his demeanor now; his eyes were beady black. Were we competing? Was this how I was going to die, fighting for this sacred space, my prayer altar, with a creature who thought I was after his mate? I remembered how people on *hanblecheya* were sometimes visited at night by coyotes, and suddenly this all seemed much too real — the shepherd's teeth sinking into my wrist, his slobber on my hands, his hot breath mingling with mine. If he were to drive me from this altar — push me out, or compel me to run away — my *hanblecheya* would be blown. But if I refused to give way, might he not kill me? I had to act, or this was going to end badly.

In a panic I slugged the dog with an uppercut to the throat and kicked him hard with the top of my bare foot in the soft space between his ribs and his genitals. He yelped and jumped off the blanket. He began circling the altar, teeth bared, clearly thinking of another approach. I heard myself say, "No, please, go away, I didn't want to hurt you, just go away, please." But he came at me again, head low, snarling. Alarmed, the bitch jumped up and ran about ten yards away. As the shepherd grabbed a leg of my sweatpants, I begged him again to retreat, pleaded with God to stop him. Desperate, I drove my fist into his jaw, then both fists into his ears. He had nearly dragged me out of the altar area when, suddenly, he let go, moved off, and started sniffing around as if I had never been of any interest at all. I watched as he followed some scent. Watched until he, with the bitch in tow, disappeared over the ridge.

It was then that I realized I was crying. Crying for a dream had begun as simply as that.

I pulled the stakes and ties of the altar upright and stood in the center of the blanket. I raised my pipe to the Thunder Beings who live in the west. I offered them the pipe, bowl first. If they were paying attention, I must have had them howling with laughter, since the idea, I learned later, was to offer them a smoke — stem first. I turned ninety degrees and raised my pipe in similar fashion to the Buffalo People in the north, then turned to the Black-Tailed Deer People in the east, then to the spirits in the south. I lifted the bowl to Grandfather Sky, dipped it to Grandmother Earth, and clutched the pipe to my chest, indicating that my offer was coming from the heart.

I went through the motions of praying. But my first attempts resembled a cold motor being awakened by a low battery; not all parts of me seemed ready yet. Did I believe in spirits? No. In beseeching them I had succeeded only in seeing myself from their point of view: a fifty-seven-year-old stoop-shouldered, bare-headed white man wearing green Gap sweatpants and a blue L. L. Bean work shirt, a key grip from New York City whose doctor had warned him to watch his cholesterol and wear a hat in the sun.

But by paying attention to the six directions and positioning my heart at the center of all things, as instructed, I had succeeded at least in *locating* myself — my physical self — there in the declivity of that hilltop in South Dakota, not far from the longitudinal center of America on north parallel forty-three. And by imagining myself at the center of all things I suddenly felt perfectly at home, since this position mimicked the way I had lived my whole self-centered life. The spotlight was on me alone now. And the sun bore down, but I raised my collar against it.

Not unlike a child kneeling by his bed, I prayed out loud for each member of my family: for my father; for my son, Chelsey, who had died twenty-six years earlier at the age of eighteen months; for my mother, who now lived alone; and for my daughter. I spoke softly, so as not to be overheard by humans, should any be lurking about. I did the directional offerings with the pipe again and prayed to be given a vision.

*Not bad,* I thought. This was going to be easier than I had expected, and praying, I found, had a calming effect on me. Proud of myself, I sat down on the hot wool blanket. A few minutes passed before the truth began to sink in — there was nothing else to do on this hill *but* pray.

My mind wandered, searching for a constructive idea to write about later. What about the alcohol problem on the reservation? Now *there* was a subject I could address in some authoritative fashion when I got down from the hill. I had kicked drugs and booze fifteen years before. Who better to speak to the issue than me? I began composing a speech to a tribal council, to a powwow of all the Indian nations. I saw myself as a significant and long-awaited messenger to the Lakota people — to *all* Native people. *So there is a purpose to my coming here,* I thought. The notion produced in me a wild exhilaration, as if at long last I had found my destiny.

Without pencil and paper to compose it, however, my speech to the powwow soon fizzled. My destiny evaporated. I grew bored. My freckled skin seemed awfully pale under the increasingly harsh sunlight. I got a sudden urge to check my phone messages and e-mail. A lot of people would be wondering about me. Several times I found myself shifting my position on the blanket and reaching for . . . what? A cell phone? A thermos of iced tea? Fruit salad? A cookie? What time was it, anyway? The sun, sitting only one hand above my new horizon, sliced in on me like a machete.

The desire to write overwhelmed me. Sitting there on the hilltop, I felt, was clearly a form of procrastination. *I should get down from this hill and start writing in my tent immediately.* I stood up, but the tobacco ties reminded me there was nowhere to run.

My first wife, Catherine, leapt into my mind. She was the mother of my two children, a woman who had actually *believed* in me and accompanied me to Spain so I could write a novel — the novel that never was. Then came my second wife, Lucille. She was the woman who had supported me while I actually *did* write a novel — the novel that never got published — and from whom I was now seeking a divorce. Then a whole slew of girlfriends — Barbara, Sandra, Betsy, Jennifer, Michou, Claire, Tabitha, Kiko — clamored to be remembered. I had professed undying love to them all, failed in love with them all.

The floodgate was open now. People I had wronged when I was drinking, people I had ignored when they were dying, people I had never thanked for helping me, people who had tolerated my worst behavior and suffered betrayal and disappointment at my hands — teachers, mentors, surrogate parents, partners, employers, employees, neighbors, passersby — I tried to keep pace with them all, praying for forgiveness from them all in one long, desperate attempt at absolution. It was like vomiting. Just when I thought I had brought them all up — thrown light on them and thus absolved myself — more faces asked to be remembered, more memories played out before my eyes. I heard a choking sob, then saw my sobbing self as if from high above.

I needed to *do* something quickly. I must have prayed for forgiveness from a hundred people already, and still new ones came to mind. I never realized I had known so many souls so intimately, and yet I had forgotten them all in the ongoing rush of my life. Just the people who had died, for God's sake! Skydiving, combat, car accidents, motorcycles, horseback riding, gunshots, alcohol, drugs, cancer, old age. Why was *I* alive? I had jumped out of airplanes, sped cars, messed around on motorcycles. I had been thrown from a horse, shot at, knifed. I had drunk myself to oblivion, snorted coke, smoked dope, dropped acid, eaten too many eggs . . . Why was I still here? What had I done to deserve being in the world right now?

I looked around. My eyes had adjusted somewhat to seeing without glasses. None of my agitation was reflected in my surroundings. A white butterfly landed gently on a black tobacco tie. Another butterfly, a monarch, settled on a nearby Scottish thistle. I remembered my grandfather telling me that I was descended from a Scottish king, and I felt oddly soothed.

Off to my left a chipmunk rustled in the brush, a crow swooped onto the limb of a nearby tree, and a bumblebee zoomed through my altar space, its buzzing the only sound on the still air. So quiet now. I measured the position of the sun again. No change. It hadn't moved an inch, but it was searing my skin more deeply with each passing second. I pulled the small camp blanket over my head, but the effect was ovenlike, so I dropped it. Tucking the pipe under one arm, I stood and removed my sweatpants and underwear. Knotting the elastic on one side of my Calvin Klein briefs, I fashioned a cap and slipped it over my head. I put on my sweatpants again and sat down.

After a while I hit on the notion of measuring time not from the now useless horizon, but backward, from the straight-up noon position. Extending my right arm I measured hand widths, from the zenith eastward to the sun. It was only half past nine! I would cook to death if this heat continued.

Despair settled in. Black Elk had his vision as a youngster. He knew from the get-go what he was about. What good was a vision at age fifty-seven? Whom would I tell it to? Who would listen? The world was full of New Age charlatans, overrun with visionaries. Who needed another one? What difference could *any* vision make to the people of New York City in the ravenous last days of the twentieth century? What was I doing here, waiting for butterflies to speak? Why had I never asked myself this simple question: What is *wrong* with you? Other men my age, friends of mine, had led purposeful, dignified lives — their accomplishments lined up like ducks in a row. Me, I was still one big question mark, still looking for the writer in myself. Well, here he was, with his underpants on his head.

Unable to see what good the prayer pipe was doing me, I put it down on the blanket and did some push-ups. I folded my small blanket into a cushion and sat on it cross-legged. A wood nymph landed on my wrist. A daddy longlegs crawled over my big toe. When my knees began to ache, I stood up stiffly and checked the sun again. Not quite noon. My lips were parched.

I felt an awful thirst, and my saliva had turned thin and foamy. I ripped off my "cap" and dropped to my knees. Folding up like an accordion, I rested my forehead on the blanket. I pushed the pipe aside, pulled up my skimpy work-shirt collar, and dangled my arms alongside my torso. This probably wasn't proper *hanblecheya* behavior, but I didn't care now. The sun had won this battle. The heat seemed to come from everywhere, even from beneath the blanket. The air, so utterly motionless, remained unresponsive to my plight. My forehead, already burned, prickled now against the rough wool.

"I give up," I said.

I could smell dog on the blanket as I faded away.

When I came out of it — woke up, if that's the word — I unfolded my body slowly into an upright seated position, my buttocks pressing into my heels. A small cloud now covered the sun, but I could tell by the glow behind the cloud that it had to be somewhere around 1:30 P.M. The butterflies were gone, the air still dead. I felt unusually alert, as if I had been wakened from an afternoon nap by a knock on the door. Some sound had caught my attention — a sound emanating from something that I now imagined to be poised close behind me. I held my breath. A chill spread from my spine and traveled across my shoulder blades and down my arms. Like a frog sensing the presence of a snake, I was stricken with apprehension. I did not dare look behind me, afraid that I might see some terrible morphing of man and beast dressed in hide and wearing war paint. I waited, blood pounding in my temples, listening for a repeat of the sound I had heard in my sleep. Then, from behind my right shoulder, came a gentle waft of air, as if someone, just once, had swiped a fan. A perfectly subtle movement of air that had nothing in common with a breeze and was not at all sustained like a breeze. Its touch was abrupt and brief, like an exhalation —

a nearly imperceptible adjustment of molecules, muscled with intent.

I grabbed the pipe, jumped to my feet, and began offering to-bacco to the directional beings as fast as I could. In my memory of it I whirled around and around, but that seems too cinematic to be true. In fact, all my self-consciousness had evaporated, so I no longer saw myself from above, as if from a camera crane, and therefore have no idea what I did or said or how I might have appeared. I do know that I trained my eyes on the sky, using only my peripheral vision to look around me, and that I saw no fierce spirit, no man or beast from which that startling sound might have emanated. But in the absence of such a manifesta-tion, I understood immediately that the disturbance, whatever it had been, was inextricably connected to my anticipation of it and that for all practical purposes it had come from within me. With this understanding, my perspective shifted completely. I was suddenly seeing the naked facts of my existence, in a way I never had before, beyond anything learned, beyond any re-membering, as if I had dropped in from some parallel universe to witness my place in the continuum of this one. I saw my fa-ther, gone on ahead of me, and my son, ahead of him. I saw how my life — all life — was fastened to Time, as if magnetically to an escalator, and that no amount of stalling or hoping or dream-ing was going to delay the dying. The dead were lost forever to the living when they went, as the living were to the dead. Unshielded by my usual rational constructs, I felt, for the first time, the ruinous sadness — cosmic and inescapable — of being human.

The sun reappeared. I licked my dry lips with my dry tongue and looked off to the south, toward the ridge over which Arturo and the dogs had disappeared. Thirst and hunger soon conspired to make a drama of this panorama. From nowhere, and attached to nothing, a gauzy curtain was drawn across my view, obscuring it. In my new frame of mind I understood this to be death's curtain, and as I continued to watch, it was drawn back again for me to see what lay beyond: nothing more than the same old view to the south. As I watched these theatrics it dawned on me that it was not going to be over when I died. Impossibly — but here it was in front of me — life carried right through death into life again. There *was* no death, no end, only endless consequences. This was it, here and now, forever. Waiting to die would get me nowhere. And dying wouldn't get me off the hook. The vision was devastating — and, worse, indelible. I knew instantly that there would be no pulling back from what I had seen, no way to undo it.

Clusters of dark brown wood nymphs landed on my bare head, hands, and arms, drawn to my salty skin as they might otherwise have been attracted to pinesap. Through sweaty eyes I squinted at the concentric gold and purple circles on their wings. I picked up the pipe and raised it to the six directions. I wanted this *hanblecheya* to be over.

Five or six more hours dragged by. The sun dipped beneath the western ridge of the bowl — my false horizon — cooling both the declivity and me, inviting me to consider more deeply what I had seen. Inviting me also to step back into my underwear.

Arturo came and fetched me just before sunset, around nine o'clock. We didn't exchange a single word. Riding down from the hill at dusk I could see smoke from the sweat lodge, a lingering swath of gold in the last rays of sunlight. We pulled up near the lodge. The same people who had been there the night before were hanging out around the fire. Mike took my blanket and pipe and told me to get in the lodge and sit on the hot seat. He crawled in behind me and closed the door flap. Just him and me, there in the dark. Only four hot rocks in the pit. He tossed a ladleful of water on the rocks.

I felt emptied of emotion. Emptied too of the illusion that I knew anything at all anymore. Fear hovered somewhere at the edge of this new void. I told Mike what I had seen while up the hill as best I could — everything except my fight with the dog, of which I felt ashamed. The words tumbled from my mouth, a string of embarrassingly inarticulate observations about how I dropped the pipe and fell asleep, how I got freaked out by something scary, how Time was an unstoppable escalator, how I wouldn't be able to find my friends and family again, how my son died long before my father did, how Death was just a curtain, and that maybe it isn't over when we die. Mike said "*Aho!*" after each observation. When I was done he told me I had gotten it exactly right — that of all the creatures on earth, human beings were the least well adapted, the latest to arrive, and the most inept. He told me a few things about the pipe I had carried — that there was both good and bad in it, just as there was good and bad in every human being.

"The way of the pipe is hard," he said. "You heard the wind speak, you did good."

When he was done, the door opened, more hot rocks were added to the pit, and everyone else crawled in.

We all staggered out an hour later and stood in a circle under the stars, sharing a smoke from the pipe I had taken up the hill. Afterward I took a drink of water and went into the Little Boy house and partook of the feast, which consisted not of bacon and eggs and pancakes and strawberries, but of boiled tripe. I nibbled at the gristly stuff but dumped most of it in the trash when no one was looking. I made a peanut butter and jelly sandwich.

I slept dreamlessly in my tent that night and awoke a little after dawn, sick at heart, as if a loved one had just died. A familiar piece of me seemed to be gone — perhaps my rational certainty that life was bracketed between birth and death, or perhaps just rationality itself. As I lay on my sleeping bag, the strange dread I had felt when first entering the reservation blossomed again. What had I been thinking, getting myself involved in this?

Arturo was still asleep in the cabin. So was the whole Little Boy household — half-naked teenagers and a few older folks, lying on the muddy linoleum floor. All beds, sofas, and easy chairs were full to capacity, and the television was still on. Young Wambli lay sprawled in his underwear on a blanket near the front door, the broken airplane tucked under his arm. I covered his bare feet.

As I brushed my teeth in the bathroom I considered folding my tent and driving home. I had finished my *hanblecheya*, done what I had come for. Besides, I had spent a lot of money already. This wasn't my world. No one would miss me. I wouldn't really ever have to come back. If I left right now, I could be in Rapid City in a few hours. I could sit down in a McDonald's and start writing. Somehow, having the option to leave made staying tolerable.

I couldn't find a coffeepot anywhere, so I waited on the front steps for someone to wake up. Underneath me, through the cracks, I could see the German shepherd and the female mutt sleeping together in the shade.

When I went inside again, Mike was up. He stood shirtless at the stove, dumping Maxwell House coffee from a large can into a pot of boiling water.

"So that's how you do it," I said.

Together we watched it brew, then dipped our cups into the mix. The stuff tasted like bitter mud. Mike sat down on the one kitchen chair, stiffly, like an old farmer. I moved to the wall and leaned against it, hoping for a heart-to-heart chat with this guy, hoping he might ease the feeling of dread that was nagging me. The TV droned in the living room, something about a rising star in Hollywood.

"So," I said.

Mike sipped his coffee then sat forward uncomfortably, adjusting his back.

"So, I got through it okay?" I said.

He nodded. Then he yawned.

"I've got to tell you," I said, "I still feel a bit spooked by my time up there."

"Yep," he said, "you will." He stuck out his bare foot and nudged a rotten onion peel across the floor, closer to the wastebasket.

"So, you're going to hold the sun dance soon?" I said.

"Yep," he said. "We got eighty trees to cut today. Gotta make some shade for the sun dance circle."

"That chain saw going to come in handy?" I asked, shamelessly fishing for a thank-you.

"Yep."

"Twenty-four-inch blade," I said. "You can cut through anything with that."

He gulped the last of his coffee, fingered the grounds on the rim of his mug, and stared long and hard at the floor.

"You think I should try the sun dance?" I asked. "Think I should get pierced sometime?"

He stood up slowly, dipped his cup into the pot, sat down again. "Up to you," he said.

I stared at him. Would I have made friends with this moody guy at a party in New York? Not likely. But he knew some things, and I had the feeling he knew something about me. I tossed my coffee grounds in the wastebasket, dipped my mug into the brew, and leaned against the wall again.

"Look at you," he said.

"What?" I said.

"You're standing there like a teenager."

"What do you mean?" I asked, taken aback.

"Ever since you pulled in with Arturo, you been standing

around, looking at the walls and the ceiling, thinking, *How am I gonna fit in around here?* You been wandering around outside, staring at the shapes of clouds and saying, 'Send me a sign. Who am I?'" He laughed. "You don't watch out, you'll end up like a guy come here last year, thought he was Crazy Horse in another life. Thought he'd come back to save the whole tribe and lead us into battle. It's pretty simple here with us Indians, you know. Look around you. Look at what needs to be done around here."

I felt a sudden surge of shame. I had no clout at all with this man. Obviously he saw me not as an educated city dweller, a man whose career in the film industry bespoke a certain acquaintance with power, but as a dense, naive wannabe, no more savvy than some starry-eyed kid barking orders on a film set.

My face grew hot. I remembered how — in the days before film schools supplied "interns" to the film business — I used to winnow the true apprentices from the herd of production assistants who aspired to work on movie sets. Whenever I spotted a new PA dreamily hanging around the camera, I would borrow a push broom from the prop department and begin sweeping the floor. I would start small and move out in an ever-widening arc, gathering cigarette butts, paper cups, gum wrappers, and such, until I got to where the PA was standing. "Excuse me," I might say, or "Don't mind me, I'll work around you," or "I hope I'm not raising too much dust for you." On occasion one of these candidates would ask if there was something he or she could do to help. Only rarely did one of them just take the broom from my hands and finish the job. But that did happen, and when it did I knew I had landed an apprentice.

"You want eggs," said Mike, "there's some in there. Bacon too, you guys brought."

"No," I said, "that's okay."

I set down my coffee cup.

I went outside and stood on the porch steps. The chain saw's carton was lying empty in the middle of the driveway. I poked around and found a busted lawn-mower cord under an empty gas can. I threw a box hitch around the middle of the carton and stood it on its end. Failing to find a rake anywhere, I got a pitchfork from the sweat lodge and began scraping into a pile all the aluminum cans, plastic bottles, rotted clothing, and Pampers. I dumped the detritus into the carton. When I had separated and set aside the salvageable tools — open-end wrenches, speed bits, a tire iron — and stacked all the plastic toys in one spot, I knelt down and secured the bottom of the carton with a seven-foot length of bailing wire.

When I looked up, I saw Wambli standing in the doorway, the broken airplane in his outstretched hand.

# 2

# Just Pears

M Y FATHER DIED in the dining room in the autumn
of 1995, sixteen months before my *hanblecheya* on
the Pine Ridge Reservation. When it became clear
that he could no longer negotiate the stairs to his bedroom, he
chose the setting for his final stand: the dining room, the smallest of the downstairs rooms. It was closest to the kitchen and
not too far from a toilet. My younger brother and I dismantled
and removed the oval mahogany table, around which our family
had gathered for meals for as long as any of us could remember,
and in its place we installed a hospital bed. We left the armoire
where it stood, shifted the highboy to the left, and rearranged
my father's oil paintings on the wall. My sister rented a standby
oxygen system and set up a makeshift nursing station consisting
of a large box of Kleenex, a mercury thermometer, a tiny blue
bottle of morphine, and a crystal vase filled with fresh dahlias.
My mother, who was struggling with dementia, gazed in wonderment and confusion at the transformation. "Oh, my!" she
said. When my father got into bed that first night, dressed in

a bright red sweatsuit (hood and all), I turned to my sister and whispered, "Here we go."

To die at home, at age eighty-six, with your family around you, is storybook stuff. Timing is key, as my father was aware. He did not want to exhaust everyone with anticipation. "You have your own lives to worry about," he said. He and my mother lived in Cross River, New York. My younger sister, Leslie, lived three hours away, in Boston; my brother, Lochlin, five hours north, in Vermont; and I, two hours east, in Connecticut. I also still had my apartment in New York City, an hour away. The three of us were free to leave our work at a moment's notice, and we wouldn't have missed his dying for all the world, but Dad got it right: we didn't want to be repeatedly gearing up for the big event.

My father had been diagnosed with prostate cancer at age seventy. Sixteen years later, in the summer of 1995, the cancer spread to the bone. Complications set in about a month later, just before he died. At the beginning of that final month, October, I was on brief leave from my film work and was finishing up a writing fellowship in Virginia. Leslie called and said she'd just taken Dad to the hospital with congestive heart failure. I told her to put him on the phone.

"What the hell is congestive heart failure?" I asked him.

He explained, between gasps for air, that it had something to do with water in the lungs. "If it isn't one thing it's another," he said. "Stay where you are, I'll wait till you get back."

When I arrived at the hospital three nights later, his young doctor, a family friend, was massaging his feet. He responded to her gentle strokes with appreciative *oooohs* and *aaahs*. Clearly, he was still having trouble breathing.

I leaned over him, kissed his bald pate, and took hold of his gnarly hand.

"Well, it looks like we're coming to the end here," he said.

"Really?" I said. The old man's grip seemed pretty strong. I glanced at the doctor. Tears were streaming down her cheeks.

"Yep," said my father, "looks like the time has come."

"How does that feel to you — coming to the end?" I asked.

"To tell you the truth," he said, pausing to catch his breath, "I'm kind of looking forward to it."

Looking forward to it? Probably no one had looked forward to death *less* than Lawrence Beall Smith. He always talked about his dying easily enough, but in fact "being in the world" was the only perspective he'd ever allowed himself. His own father, an ardent Midwestern Methodist, had ruined him for religion and thus for the promise (and perspective) of an afterlife. "Life lives on in art," my father would say, "and in the memory of others." With this conviction, he managed, until the last month of his life, to forestall the deeper considerations: How would he *know* if his art lived on? And, how, *exactly,* might he be remembered? Even I, at age fifty-five and with no artistic track record, had been seized with fear by such considerations. So I kept a sharp eye on my father for any fissures that might develop in his veneer of stoicism.

His propensity to ignore or delay the serious stuff permeated his being and presented to those around him the portrait of an upbeat, singular man who had carved out for himself a nearly picture-perfect artist's life: working at home, raising a family, being his own boss. For me, as a teenager during the 1950s, his carefully crafted world had felt claustrophobic — the antithesis of being "on the road." His stoic refusal (out of step with the zeitgeist of the time) to give vent to misery, anger, or complaint, or to respond directly to my own venting, seemed to me like weakness, not strength. He was of a mind to let unpleasant things blow over, which meant that his response to emotional outbursts was often silent and thus open to interpretation. Rather than try to parse my father's unsaid words, I gravi-

tated toward my more forthcoming mother, Winn. A visual artist herself, and a big fan of Carl Jung, she appreciated metaphor
and provided psychological context to complex emotions. She
saw shadows where my father saw light. Predictably, the silent
tension between my father and me had ballooned quite early,
and it carried well into my adult life. It mellowed only after I
quit drinking and married for the second time and bought a
house and land, as he had done. And by the time I got around to
investigating my own inadequacies as a father, I'd long since for-
given — and perhaps had even grown to admire — his stoicism.

When it came time for my father to die, however, it seemed
critical not just to honor his life and his art, but also to discover
what he had *meant* by his life and art.

With the help of potassium pills, the water left his lungs, and after a few days I drove my father home from the hospital. Instead
of stopping at the house, where the dining room was all set up
for him, I pulled the car up to his painting studio, a converted
barn that stood several hundred feet from the main house. "You
probably want to get back to work," I said.

I helped him out of the car, steadied him across a patch of
gravel, and eased him through the studio door. Once inside, he
just stood there, stock-still. He looked at the cavernous space
where for fifty years he'd painted book illustrations and por-
traits, and churned out lithographs and etchings. A cold north-
ern light washed over the easel, on which rested an upside-
down painting of a single daffodil. The west wall was covered
with thumbtacked photos of his children and grandchildren, all
of whom he'd painted or sculpted at one time or another. One of
these, a faded black-and-white eight-by-ten of my daughter and
me, had been on that wall for twenty years. The place smelled
of turpentine, linseed oil, and, though my father hadn't smoked
a pipe since the 1970s, tobacco.

He frowned at his surroundings, as if they constituted another man's space, then shook his head and turned back toward the door. When he failed to check the thermostat or even glance at the pile of gallery announcements, I understood that it was over for him — the performance of art. His life's occupation (he'd never had an ordinary job) no longer stood between him and the end of life itself. My heart sank, looking at him.

"It's okay," he said, on our slow walk toward the house. "Don't you think it's okay?"

"It's up to you. The studio's not going anywhere."

"Who's going to win the World Series?"

"Cleveland's my guess," I said.

"I don't know," he said. "Atlanta's got that pitcher, Tom Glavine."

Leslie took over the following morning, and I returned to my house in Connecticut. My second marriage was unraveling. We had no children together, my wife and I, and our work was taking us in different directions. She was away, and so, alone, I supervised the final week of roof shingling. I put the vegetable and flower gardens to bed for the winter, painted the south side of the garage, raked up the last of the leaves, and winterized the pickup truck, the tractor, and the riding mower. Then I packed a couple of bags and moved into our apartment in New York City, by myself.

A few days later, I visited my father and found Leslie reading to him from Sogyal Rinpoche's *The Tibetan Book of Living and Dying*. "The painful bardo of dying falls between the moment we contract a terminal illness or condition that will end in death, and the ceasing of the 'inner respiration.'" In deference to my arrival, she closed the book, patted my father's hand, and left the room to help Hilda, the housekeeper, make some lunch.

"How about that!" my father said. "I'm in the bardo of dying!"

I pulled up a chair beside his bed. He seemed as feisty as ever, though noticeably thinner in the face. We entered into the obligatory ritual of small talk. He asked about the weather in Connecticut, and I inquired about the status of their house and grounds. Did the storm windows need washing? Had anyone cleaned the roof gutters? Were any Brussels sprouts left in the garden? I knew, of course, that I was talking to a man for whom these concerns were no longer pressing, but I didn't know how else to converse with him. As we bantered back and forth about the fine art of window caulking, it dawned on me that I too was now a man for whom these topics of male domesticity were of no concern. I'd left all that behind. Then, by some unspoken agreement, we dropped the subject. A silence ensued. I stared past my father, out the window at the reservoir bed across the road. This normally large body of water had been drained months earlier to facilitate repairs to the dam, four miles away. Brown swamp grass waved in the breeze where once the water had been.

I turned to the small oil painting hanging over the bed. Three yellowish green Bartlett pears lay on an orange-pink cloth, set against a dove gray background. The pear on the right sat squarely on its bottom, which perfectly resembled a woman's buttocks. The fat pear on the left tilted a little — on one cheek, as it were. A tall skinny pear stood in the middle, favoring its right cheek. You could feel the texture of the pears and sense the softness within, at the points where the skin dimpled and turned brown. It was not a still life so much as a dance.

"All three pears have stems," I said.

My father gave me a puzzled look.

"How long did it take you to paint that?"

"Days," he said.

"Why three?" I asked.

"I didn't say it took three days," he said.

"I mean pears — why three pears? The Trinity comes to mind, no?" I smiled.

My father frowned. "What are you talking about?"

Again, I studied the painting. "Seriously," I said. "Why not four pears? Or five? Why Bartlett and not Bosc?"

"Because," he said, "that's what was lying around."

"But why did you paint them?"

He shrugged.

"Maybe the pears are your kids," I suggested.

Again he shrugged, this time with a flash of annoyance in his eyes. I noticed him looking at my left hand, at the lack of a wedding band.

"Like it or not," I said, "art has a kind of iconography — produced by the artist, or perceived by the viewer."

He nodded, guarded and suspicious.

"So those pears could be anything. The Father, the Son, and the Holy Ghost . . . or your own children . . . or the third season of life . . ."

"Or just pears," he said.

"No," I said, "not *just* pears. We bring something else to the experience of looking at pears, don't we?"

Silence. My father appeared as annoyed with me then as he'd ever been, and I, in turn, as frustrated.

"Listen, I know what those pears mean to *me*," I said. "But why did *you* paint them — instead of turning on a ball game or taking a walk or having a martini?"

I felt like a wolf circling a weakened sheep. I couldn't control myself.

Hilda, my parents' Ecuadoran housekeeper, came through the swinging door, holding a tray with four bowls of chicken soup. My sister followed with a plate of toasted English muffins. My mother passed out cloth napkins, and we sat in dining room chairs around the bed, while Hilda served my father and then put bowls on our laps.

"*Gracias*, Hilda," I said. "*Es la mejor sopa de pollo en todo el mundo. La propia vida de mi padre. Gracias.*"

Hilda looked at my father and put her arm around my shoulders. "He speak such good Spanish!"

My father ignored her compliment.

I visited twice more that week, and then again on what turned out to be the day before he died. The night I arrived, November 1, I found him dancing in the living room with Hilda. My mother sat on the sofa, laughing gaily at the scene. I stood in the vestibule, looking in, listening: Mozart's Violin Sonata no. 6 in G Major. My brother and sister watched from the shadows at the far end of the living room. As a young man, my father had looked a bit like Fred Astaire and shared a similar lightness of step. He moved stiffly now, with pain, but the allegro dance momentarily unveiled his youthful self — just long enough to evoke and emphasize the kind of spirit that was about to pass.

The next morning, after making me bacon, eggs, and pancakes, Hilda told me that my father didn't want breakfast. This was a first. I went to his bedside.

"You don't want to eat?"

He shook his head, avoiding my eyes.

"Eat," I said.

Again he shook his head. I touched his forehead with the palm of my hand and felt the rude hardness of his skull. He didn't have a fever.

"It's a beautiful day," I said. "How about a little walk to work up an appetite?"

He eased himself out of bed. I tied his red sweatpants and helped him put on his socks and sneakers. I wrapped a blue scarf around his neck and got him into a green nylon jacket and a purple wool cap. Then I walked him out through the kitchen and onto the back patio. The morning sun was bright and warm.

"Let's sit," he said, stopping beside one of the steel patio chairs.

I sat next to him. We shared a view of the backyard and the pasture beyond it. The maples and oaks and honey locusts were bare, and the leaves on the ground had turned a uniform brown. A tall, dead pine tree rose in the middle of the pasture, its straggly crown of limbs a perch for raptors.

"So, Dusty," he said, "how do you think I've done?"

"What do you mean?" I asked.

He indicated the property, the house, the barn, my mother's studio across the driveway. "All this, and you kids. Did I do okay?"

"You did great," I said.

"You know, when I got out of college, I had an offer to study with Hans Hofmann, in Provincetown. Uncle Harold gave me the money."

"And?" I said. I'd heard this story before.

"I met your mother. All it took was one look. We used that money for our honeymoon in Europe."

"How might things have worked out if you'd studied with Hofmann?"

"Oh, I don't know," he said.

"Your paintings might be more abstract."

"Never cared for abstract," he said. And then he asked, "Did I do the right thing?"

"You tell me."

"I have no regrets," he said.

"You wouldn't hurt my feelings if you did," I said. "Ambition and family are a hard mix."

"I never expected to be famous. We've had sixty wonderful years together, your mother and I."

It wasn't lost on me that none of us kids had been able to sustain our first marriage — or me, now, my second.

"It's different for everyone," said my father, as if he had read my mind. "The timing, and how it all turns out. We can't really know. We have an idea, but we can't really know."

A small squadron of crows landed on the lawn and began making a huge racket. My father frowned at the intrusion. "Thieves!" he said.

I watched the large black birds strutting about, pecking at autumn remains.

"Five crows," I said.

"Look at that over there." My father pulled himself forward in his seat. "What *is* that bush? I prune it every spring. It's always the last bit of color every year — always in November."

The bush, a small euonymus, or spindle tree, stood in a little clearing just beyond my mother's studio.

"Let's go see it," he said, trying to stand up. I took hold of his arm and walked him slowly across the driveway.

We stood next to the spindle tree, staring at its flame-shaped crimson leaves. He reached out a shaky hand and pointed his index finger — not at a colorful leaf but at one of the branches. Round, and covered with a light gray bark, the branch had four sharp ridges running the length of it. The branch in cross section looked like a circle with four equally spaced spikes on its circumference, suggesting the corners of an imaginary square. Suddenly, I remembered reading that in medieval alchemy, the attainment of true knowledge requires learning how to "square the circle." The problem of squaring the circle — constructing a square equal in area to a given circle — is famously resistant to a purely geometric solution. Which is why the alchemists (those who would transform lead into gold) chose the metaphor to describe the nearly impossible task of bringing together, and holding as one, the worldly domain and the domain of the spirit. For the artist or writer, I now thought, that would mean the task of combining the literal and figurative elements of imagery. It would require being able to see the symbolic as real, and the real as symbolic — all at once, but quietly. I touched the branch my father pointed to, then closed my hand around it, pressing its four sharp ridges into my palm. Our eyes met.

"Thanks," I said. "I'd never noticed this before."

"Think nothing of it," he answered.

I took a long walk before lunch, and when I returned, my brother, sister, and mother were sitting at the kitchen table, eating soup with Hilda. They spoke in hushed tones. A place was set for me.

"Dad's not hungry," Lochlin told me.

"I just read to him about the essences," whispered Leslie. She was talking about Sogyal Rinpoche's "seven thought states resulting from ignorance and delusion" that are brought to an end at the moment of death.

"Your reading seems to be helping him," I said, sitting down.

But as I started to eat with my family, I imagined my father lying alone in his bed in the next room, and then I imagined him imagining us. Without saying anything, I stood up and took my soup into the dining room, letting the swinging door shut behind me. My father was reclining at a forty-five-degree angle, staring at the ceiling. I pulled up a chair and sat at the foot of his bed. I dunked my English muffin in the soup and took a bite. He looked at me. I offered him a taste. He neither nodded nor shook his head, but stared straight at me. For just a moment, I felt I had made a terrible mistake. My brother and sister, after all, had remained respectfully in the kitchen. Here I sat, demonstrating my appetite for life. It must have seemed to my father that I was rubbing it in — that I could eat and he could not, that I was going on with life and he was not. A look of pained betrayal overtook his face. It was all I could do to swallow. But I kept staring at him and slurping my soup, until finally, after about a minute, he turned to gaze out the window at the bare-limbed maples. Shards of sunlight struck his face. He shut his eyes and began to nap.

Hilda's urging brought us together at the end. *"Mira,"* she said. *"Es importante.* The time is close." At six o'clock, we converged in the dining room and took up positions around the bed. In spite of sharp back pain, my father had refused morphine all day.

"It makes me feel fuzzy," he said.

My brother cranked the bed up, slowly, so Dad could see us all clearly.

"Well, Winnie," he said to my mother, "this is it." He took her hand and kissed it.

Then he turned to me. "Is it okay to go now?" He was smiling.

"Yes," I said.

"Are you sure? You'll all be okay?"

We said that we would, and we each touched him, in our turn.

He signaled us to lower the bed. Then he closed his eyes, and within the hour, died.

# 3

# Meeting at the Water's Edge

---

I MUST HAVE BEEN expecting the beast for years. How else, I ask myself now, could I have known with such certainty, and at one hundred yards, that the slate-gray creature clawing its way across my lawn was a snapping turtle? At that distance it would have been hard to distinguish a kettle from a skillet. But when I saw the thing, I bolted out of my lawn chair like a man who'd sat on a tack. It was moving from the pasture toward the pond as irrevocably as an M-60 tank, which accounts perhaps for the odd sensation it produced in me: that I was watching something both hopelessly inevitable and utterly intolerable.

When I was a boy, snapping turtles were spoken of with the kind of awe usually reserved for legendary bank robbers. Poking around the edges of the reservoir, near where I grew up, my friend Lewis and I regularly reinforced the awesome reputation of the snapper.

"It'll chomp on your big toe while you're skinny-dipping at night!" he'd say.

"Yeah, and you're lucky if it's only your toe!" I'd say.

"Once it bites you, it never lets go, not even if you cut off its head!"

On our rounds, we would occasionally glimpse one of those ominous armor-plated shells nosing like a submarine into the sun-streaked depths near the shoreline. Did we ever actually meet a snapper, face to face? No.

But when I finally encountered one in 1992, on the expansive lawn of the country house my second wife and I owned in northeast Connecticut, I was hurling obscenities at it: "You motherfucker, you sonofabitch." I threw down my *New York Times* and stepped into my open-toed sandals. "Don't you dare go in my pond, you prick!"

The turtle, unable to decipher my command, continued to advance. I figured I could hold it at bay, prevent it from reaching the pond, where my neighbors' kids swam on weekends. But I needed help — someone to fetch my hard-toed boots, my work gloves, a weapon of some kind, or a cardboard box. My wife was working in the city. The nearest neighbor lived a quarter-mile down the road. There wasn't any help.

A long-handled edging tool protruded from a nearby peony bed, its crescent-shaped steel blade rusted from disuse. Grabbing it, I started across the lawn, closing on the turtle at an angle. If it saw me coming, it didn't let on, acting instead as if it owned the place — and worse yet, as if it was accustomed to walking this way. "Hey, you!" I yelled, breaking into a run, clutching the edger in my fist, the way an aborigine might clutch a spear, but with none of the confidence. Already my heart was pounding. Already I knew my reluctance to hunt.

Once, at age nine, I lay prone on my family's lawn and trained the sight of my new hair-trigger air rifle on a rabbit that had wandered from the safety of a forsythia bush. I followed its movements, holding my breath as I'd been taught, but my trigger finger froze, and the rabbit bounded out of view. Perhaps in compensation for this early weakness, while working on a Nevada ranch at age seventeen I shot so many jackrabbits (my job for the day) that their carcasses outnumbered the beer cans in the pickup bed. But that killing spree was an aberration, really. In my early thirties, I purchased a hunting rifle and took it on a camping trip. I fired it twice at a tree, then ditched it under a log. In Texas, before I turned forty, I bought a holstered .357 Magnum from a broke Mexican. Strapping it on my hip, I practiced quick-draw in front of the hotel room mirror, but I never did work up the gumption to buy ammunition for it — unwilling, as it turned out, to cross the line that separates fantasy from reality. More recently, however, I'd taken a broom and swatted the daylights out of a bat I'd judged to be rabid.

When I intersected the turtle's projected path, I stopped and waited, my mouth dry, my gut tensing. The pond sat twenty feet behind me, like an untended goal.

"Get back, you!" I demanded.

The snapper, oblivious, kept moving. Fifty feet . . . thirty feet . . . twenty . . . fifteen . . . This thing was *big*, eighteen inches across at least, and clearly of another era — definitely not New Age. Not a trace of subtlety or sophistication in its four-legged gait. At ten feet, my open-toed sandals began a kind of involuntary shuffle. I raised the edger, as if fully prepared to strike.

"Back off, or else!" I ordered.

Treating me as if I were a mere inanimate object, like a rock, the creature came within two feet of my feet before it suddenly swerved — hurtled, really — to my right, like a running back eluding a tackler. I jumped in front of it, but the turtle's hind legs thrust relentlessly, its forelegs countering my every move. Head lowered, mouth agape, it backed me toward the pond. With its low center of gravity, the turtle seemed to own the horizontal plane; my height meant nothing. I don't know what it wanted more — water, or the taste of some species that lived in water — but it wanted it on some ultimately inarguable level. This wasn't going to be about negotiation. This turtle, with no respect for boundaries, no inkling that I held title to this land, no sensitivity to the anger that had built up in me long before this moment arrived, kept coming at me — until, that is, I brought the edger down one inch in front of its bluntly jutted nose.

The big advantage of being a turtle and having a shell, I had thought, was that you could hunker down and hide until your enemy went away. Or until your enemy lifted you gently by your shell, placed you in a cardboard box with air holes in it, and took you to an animal shelter, or someone else's pond — or a swamp. But this turtle took one look at the edging tool half sunk in the dirt in front of its nose, and rather than demonstrate surprise or shrink from the blade, it affected a curmudgeonly expression. With its downturned mouth and its too-steady gaze, it looked more pissed off than a bass.

Then, it *bit* the edger.

It isn't possible, of course, that a snapping turtle's beak could produce a clang by chomping on a half-buried piece of steel, but *clang* is what I heard, as surely as if two broadswords had clashed midair. The turtle removed its beak from the steel, but much too slowly, confirming those childhood prophecies and deciding for me what I could not decide for myself: that this was my job, that the buck stopped here, that to transport a creature with this kind of behavior to anyone else's pond or lawn or swamp would be irresponsible.

"That's it," I said. Realizing the implications of this standoff, I assigned the turtle a gender. "That's it for you, old boy."

Knowing what I had to do, however, was different from choosing the specific method. Should I drive the edger through

the turtle's shell, or should I decapitate the beast? His shell resembled Godzilla's hide — dense and hard, as if tempered in a
forge and capable of withstanding bazookas and rockets. His
spiked prehensile tail seemed equally formidable. His neck, as
thick as a chicken's, was a different matter. The tight skin, gray
with a yellowish tint and encrusted with tubercles, appeared
vulnerable. The trouserlike skin on his legs looked much the
same.

But where was the turtle's heart? I didn't know.

I poked his shell with the edger. His neck lengthened, and
he scowled at me, his visage suddenly shape-shifting to that of
a rattlesnake, then a hawk, then back to turtle again. Then he
just got downright impudent, like a homeless man I had seen
in Central Park during my last trip to the city. The fellow, upon
discovering me sitting on his favorite bench, reached into his
sweatpants, grabbed his balls, and shook them at me. When the
turtle shook his balls at me — biting the steel once more, and
this time hanging on — I yanked the edger free and tested his
neck with the steel.

There comes a time when you don't need more information.
I, having arrived at this juncture, knew enough. The snapper, in
his stillness, also seemed to know enough. His head drew back
into its sheath like a penis into its foreskin. His yellow eyes, en-
cased in wattles, stared out at me with a beady terror. I raised the
blade like a guillotine and waited for him to offer himself up.

I can't say whether the tears commenced at that moment
— as he began to present his neck — or as the edger actually
started to descend. But I can say that when I plunged the rusty,
cleaverlike blade down onto the turtle's neck, a cry of anguish
escaped my mouth. Everything I thought I knew about myself
— that I owned land, that I'd landed on my feet, that despite
a decade of low-life behavior, I'd finally achieved some dignity
— all that brittle artifice shattered with the first blow.

Looking down, I saw that the edger's dull blade had grazed the turtle's flat reptilian head, scalping him deeply. A hunk of bloody skin hung from his face like a wood shaving from a vise. "Oh, God," I moaned, seeing what I'd done — and what I still had left to do. Twice, three times, I sucked in air, phlegm rattling in the back of my throat. Words of some kind struggled to break through and express remorse, but they came out strangled, as once more I raised the blade and brought it down, slamming it this time onto the shell, to no effect at all.

Desperate, I tried using the edger the way it was meant to work on grass — positioning it first, then stepping down hard on it to make the cut. But the snapper would not sit still for that. I stepped back, needing time to think. When I moved forward again, the turtle strained his bloody neck and stared up at me, one eye still intact. And that's when I saw past his affect, past his "arrogance" and "impudence," past what I was projecting onto him, and I saw instead an ancient and, so help me God, *wise* creature. Suddenly, I saw whose place this was originally — whose lawn, whose pond, whose woods, whose dignity. And I just couldn't believe what I'd done.

I finished him off, the old boy. I was pathetic in the process, sobbing, moaning, gagging. He looked a mess at the end. He crawled about without a head, his old heart, wherever it resided, sustaining him nearly until dusk. While he was still kicking, I placed him on a large granite boulder, which had been hauled from the earth when the house on that land was built, back in 1710. Eventually, he ceased all movement, and I carried his carcass across the road on a coal shovel, dumping it where I wouldn't have to be constantly reminded of this encounter.

When I think of him now, my snapping turtle, I remember his beseeching eye, wincing with each whack but recovering enough between blows to communicate this to me: *You're mine.*

# 4

# The Pipe

_____

The observer's choice of what he shall
look for has an inescapable consequence
for what he shall find.

— JOHN ARCHIBALD WHEELER

ONE SUMMER DAY in 1979, my father called me and
asked if I could help him find the well that supplied
the rusty old water spigot located in the middle of
his studio garden. His studio had no interior plumbing and sat
quite some distance from the well next to the main house. With
no water pump in or around the studio, the water source for this
isolated but still-working spigot had long been a family mystery.

"It's time we got to it, don't you think?" my father said.

"I'll give it a whirl," I told him, and the following weekend I
showed up from New York City with my tools in hand: a plastic
divining rod and a stainless steel pendulum attached to a bit of
string.

I was, at the time, a thirty-nine-year-old drunk. When I

wasn't working on a movie set, I could usually be found at my local bar on the Upper West Side, drinking Jack Daniel's from a beer mug and sucking on Marlboros. Psychiatric literature would probably have it that I was medicating my pain. I prefer to think that I was agitating it. In any case, the pain I was either medicating or agitating was rooted in such profound self-ignorance that getting shit-faced just made things more interesting. At home, I smoked dope and rolled the I Ching coins nightly. I snorted large amounts of cocaine, managing to induce periodic nervous breakdowns, from which I would then recover — with the help of hatha yoga and homegrown alfalfa sprouts — so that I could resume the agitation again. The deeper I wandered into the alcoholic fog, the more convinced I became that I was about to encounter my true self. I pored over books on ESP, astrology, and pyramids. I became obsessed with alchemy and the idea of turning lead into gold. Which is how I began to practice the art of divination.

My relationship to the truth was both tenuous and self-serving. I knew it even then, the way all drinkers do. I championed any evidence that supported the paranormal — that confirmed my own divinatory powers — and I ignored my many failures, as well as any evidence that suggested such stuff was pure bunk.

I offer this confession as a disclaimer. Even after giving up booze, drugs, and cigarettes, I remain steadfastly unreliable as a scientist. I am not an impartial authority on divination. If you don't already trust that a dowsing (divining) rod is a Y-shaped instrument that sometimes reacts with what feels like an otherworldly force, in response, say, to a search for water; or if you aren't aware that the age-old practice of dowsing is still prevalent in rural and Native American communities, as well as in parts of Europe, Asia, and Africa; or if you simply cannot buy the idea that a pendulum, when suspended over a map, can be used to locate objects or minerals buried in the area the map depicts, then there's just no helping it: I'm not the one to present the subject for your consideration. If something happens only once, that's proof enough for me. If I am the only witness to it, that too will do. I'm a big fan of anomalies.

That said, let me attest that before visiting my father that weekend, I'd been having some success with the dowsing rod. Though I missed at least 50 percent of the time, I'd been able, occasionally, to find things. Like the time my girlfriend lost an earring at my place and I detected its presence not in the jumble of bed sheets or in the creases of the sofa, but in the hallway, stuck to her woolen scarf, which she'd stuffed into the sleeve of her overcoat.

Not impressed?

How about the time I was sitting at a bar with a prop man, after a long day filming a commercial? The guy was telling me about his plans to purchase a certain building lot in Brewster, New York. I happened to be idly dangling my pendulum over the bar, when suddenly I felt a shift in the way it swung. "Don't buy that land," I warned. "There's no water on it." This prediction was confirmed a few months later by some unfortunate person who *did* purchase the land. I never had to pay for my drinks in the prop man's presence again.

Still not impressed?

How about the time — six months after this story takes place — when I participated in a search for a young couple who were said to be one month behind schedule on their sailing honeymoon? Using a world map, a photograph of the couple, a sample of the woman's handwriting, and a pendulum, I concluded (correctly, as it turned out) that their forty-foot sloop had gone down off the coast of Libya, and that the couple had died.

I know. The practice of divination does not stand up to rigid examination; it is boneless, slippery stuff.

. . .

My father's outdoor spigot would be my first field test with the pendulum — a device that can be used outdoors only on a windless day. We knew where the spigot was, and we knew water fed it from *somewhere* — a nice set of givens. If my dowsing efforts failed, I could always dig straight down from the spigot, then follow the feeder pipe out to the source. But that would be a messy, exhausting alternative.

With my father standing nearby, I positioned myself at the spigot, dangled the pendulum out in front of me, and said to it, "Please point me in the direction of the water pipe." The pendulum, after an erratic start, began to swing steadily on a north-south axis. Since the studio was located just north of the spigot — at my back — I began walking south, checking my path with the pendulum every ten feet or so, the way one might navigate with a compass in the woods. When I came to a stone retaining wall, I climbed it and continued on.

Within minutes I was standing at the edge of the small pasture — an acre of fallow land that separated my family's house from adjacent county land. Back in the 1940s, my younger sister had grazed her pony in that pasture. I'd dug foxholes there, imitating scenes my father had painted in Normandy, after the invasion. My pals and I had fired BB guns, shot arrows, and heaved sod hand grenades at one another out there in the center, where a clump of honeysuckle now grew. When I was a teenager, I'd mowed and raked that field with haying equipment borrowed from a neighboring farmer.

"Remember that?" I asked my father. "Remember that beat-up old Allis-Chalmers tractor and the rusty old hay rake you had to sit on to operate it?"

"I do," said my father.

"Who mows it now?" I asked.

"Someone bush-hogs it," he said.

I looked toward the main house, the nineteenth-century,

flat-roofed dwelling I'd grown up in. My mother stood at the kitchen window, watching us.

"You know," I said, "this seems an unlikely reach for a simple run of water pipe. But it *is* downhill from here to the spigot."

"Gravity fed, you think?" asked my father.

I shrugged.

It felt good to be talking with him like this. Our relationship had been strained for years, as long as I'd been drinking and using drugs. I deferred to the pendulum again: "Tell me, am I still on the path of the pipe?"

The pendulum began a very distinct clockwise rotation (this means "yes" in pendulumese). I steadied its swing.

"The answer is in the question," I told my father, trying to give the process some dignity. I held out the pendulum again and asked: "Should I continue in this direction?"

"Oh, yes!" said the pendulum.

I took small steps now, trying to focus on the water pipe. My childhood memories of the pasture were interfering with my dowsing instincts. I fought a growing suspicion that something other than the water pipe was drawing me toward that clump of honeysuckle in the center of the pasture, a hundred feet away. Was this path a transparently emotional journey? Did I maybe just want to dig in the earth again, get down in it and hide, like a child playing soldier?

I stopped, took a deep breath, told myself to focus on the project at hand. I did my best to silence metaphorical thought. The most successful dowsers, I'd learned, were simple folk, uncomplicated by personal agendas, ulterior motives, or financial gain.

I began again, having convinced myself that I had nothing invested in this search — not the approval of my father, not some larger abstract meaning, not even an emotional lift. All I wanted was the simple truth: the source of water in my father's garden. To get there, I told myself, I must locate the water pipe. My search might end right here, or in the next town over. I was open to *any* answer, without preconception.

My father, who'd been standing at a respectful distance, struck a match on his jeans and lit his pipe. I could hear the to-bacco sizzle as he sucked the flame toward it.

"I have no preconceptions," I said out loud.

"Think *pipe*," suggested my father.

"*Shhhh*," I said. "Every search begins in darkness. I have no preconceptions. I am looking for the water pipe, the water pipe, the water pipe, the water pipe . . ."

This mantra worked for about fifteen more steps. Then I was interrupted by the thought of making a fool of myself in front of my parents. I'd carried this too far, and I was going to wind up at the honeysuckle — a middle-aged prodigal come home to slobber over his roots.

I took a deep breath and started walking again. Abruptly I stopped. The pendulum had begun swinging wildly.

"What?" asked my father.

"Wouldn't we have seen some evidence of a well out here, years ago?" I asked. I was stalling, though, to give myself time to think. I'd ceased walking because it had suddenly occurred to me that if water was symbolic of life, then I was out here in this pasture asking for the source of life — specifically for the source of the artist's life. My hidden agenda, then, was not so much to revisit my childhood as it was to discover a way to be-gin again, to change the direction of my life. *What will it take to begin again?* My silent question had provoked the pendulum in a way I'd never felt before. I'd lost all control. Embarrassed, I cupped the device in my fist.

My father took a few puffs, his brow furrowed in puzzle-ment. He was up for this, and I liked him for it.

"Ask it," he said, pointing at my closed fist.

The sun was high and hot, the air as still as in a windowless room.

I released the pendulum to dangle from its string.

"Tell me," I said, my mind struggling unsuccessfully to exclude my silent question, "am I still on the path of the pipe?"

An immediate clockwise rotation.

"Am I standing directly over the pipe?"

"Yes."

"I mean, *seriously*, am I standing over the goddamn water pipe *right now?*"

"Yes."

"Okay," I said, "we'll see about that." I planted both feet on the spot, nodded to my father. He fetched the pickax and spade from the garden.

While he watched, I dug. The earth was relatively soft, punctuated with small stones. It felt like heaven to be penetrating this ground. At a depth of about two feet, I began digging more gently, to protect the pipe from damage, should I hit it. The soil had changed in color from black to brown. The stones were bigger, harder to extract. I removed my T-shirt. My father seemed amused at my sweaty labor.

"You laugh," I said.

At a depth of three feet, I took a breather and asked the pendulum: "Are you *sure* the water pipe is here?"

"Quite sure," came the answer. And again the silent question, unbidden, loomed large in my mind: *What will it take to begin again?* The pendulum swung so hard, it nearly flew from my fingers.

"I'll go down another foot," I said, "to get below the frost line."

Then, just as I plunged the spade into the soil, I felt something softer and less resonant than rock. I lay down on my stomach, reached into the hole, and began scooping out loose earth with my bare hands. Working carefully, I exposed an inch or two of corroded water pipe. I could hardly believe it. When I began digging beneath it, it came loose from the dirt — not the imagined feeder pipe, leading from a well to the spigot. Not the logical conclusion to our search. Just a busted-off scrap of water pipe, about five inches long, with an elbow fitting at one end. An old-fashioned hunk of plumbing, attached to nothing at all, out in the middle of nowhere, with no explanation — or instructions — attached.

I lifted the specimen out of the hole for my father to see.

"Well, how 'bout that!" he exclaimed. "A pipe!"

I weighed the pipe in my hand. "It's lead," I said.

"Yep," he said. "Lead."

Without another word, and without ever referring to the water spigot again, we filled in the hole and joined my mother for lunch.

# 5

# One Day

---

But it took him a long time
Finally to make his mind up to go home.

— ELIZABETH BISHOP, "The Prodigal"

WHEN I WOKE UP, I found myself standing naked on the second-floor balcony of the motel. I gripped the metal railing like a deranged Caesar and prepared to address the populace. Looking out over the dimly lit parking lot, I realized there was not a soul in sight. I checked my wristwatch, then assessed the situation. For some reason, being naked outdoors at 4 A.M. seemed less significant than what I needed to say to the people. But I couldn't quite recall the precise message. Within this mental vacuum, the nature of my predicament began to take shape.

I looked over my shoulder and saw that the door to my room was closed. Reflexively, I patted my bare thighs, feeling for a room key. I tested the door, twisting the knob with both hands, to no effect. It was locked. It wouldn't do to kick the door in, not with bare feet. Not with the star of the movie asleep in the room next to mine. No way I could just walk into the motel office and ask for a key. I would be fired for sure.

I walked along the balcony, weighing my options. I began to imagine the news spreading on the movie set that morning. How the key grip from New York had been arrested at dawn by the Georgia State Police, charged with wandering about naked in the middle of the night; how blood tests had revealed an alcohol level like none ever recorded before; how further tests had found evidence of a nearly lethal mixture of drugs.

Deciding to seek help from a fellow crew member, I padded down the concrete stairs, my head pounding, my mouth desert dry. I banged on door 11. Hearing only a muffled voice coming from inside, I knocked harder. "Just a minute," yelled Joe, "just a minute!" Joe was the gaffer; we had gotten high together some hours earlier. I heard a toilet flush. I waited. The toilet flushed again. I pounded even harder. The toilet flushed a third time. Joe opened the door, fully dressed and prepared for a bust.

"I need a towel," I said.

The problem with being a drunk — and this is something I could not possibly have guessed at the time — is that even when you stop drinking, the fact that you were a drunk will forever intrude not only on others' assessment of you, but your own. It is impossible to write about that time in 1976, when I helped film a movie on Flannery O'Connor's farm in Milledgeville, Georgia, without first acknowledging that I was too much of a drunk to have read anything she had written — including the short story we were filming. For a key grip this would normally be an unnecessary confession; grip work is technical and has nothing to do with story line or meaning. But I was, at the time, a thirty-five-year-old man with a dream of being a writer. To be sure, years of drunken procrastination had transformed that dream into a kind of ongoing, evermore, weather-beaten expectation. Lacking any evidence that I actually was a writer and having failed enough at it to suggest that I wasn't, I had retreated to the high ground: I simply assumed I already *was* a writer. After all, if I could observe what I observed of life, and in such a brilliant way, wasn't my success a foregone conclusion? Drinking fueled this assumption, revved it up nicely each night — then drove it straight into a tree. Every morning as I kneeled at the toilet to puke up green bile, I knew I had gone another day without writing. I had taken notes perhaps, while sitting at the bar — shameless observations of humans at the trough, scribbles whose chief purpose had been to make me appear intelligent while I sucked down bourbon and chased it with beer. But while a few fortunate synaptic collisions might have produced an idea or two, those ideas — either unreadable in daylight or incomprehensible to the sober mind — were destined for the trash.

So this is what I brought to the experience of standing on a great American writer's home soil: a perverse and energetic dimness. Not that O'Connor herself noticed. Having been faithful to her art until the very end, she had succumbed to lupus twelve years earlier, at age thirty-nine. But had she lived, she may very well have found my presence fitting, since dimness, and the way it forestalls redemption, were O'Connor's trademark themes.

We were filming *The Displaced Person*, a story set in the rural South after World War II. Provincial ignorance, pettiness, and greed rule the lives of the central characters. A widow, Mrs. McIntyre (played by Irene Worth), hires an immigrant Polish farm laborer, with an eye to replacing her dairy foreman, Mr. Shortley (Lane Smith). Seeing how eagerly the Pole works, she imagines hiring more foreigners to replace her two lazy Negroes, Astor (Robert Earl Jones) and Sulk (Samuel L. Jackson). Shortley and his wife (Shirley Stoler) conspire to get rid of the Pole. No one wins. Mrs. Shortley dies suddenly. The Pole is not-so-accidentally run over and killed by his own tractor. Mrs. McIntyre herself suffers a paralyzing stroke. Mr. Shortley and the Negroes move away. A priest, Father Flynn (John Houseman), whose advice Mrs. McIntyre has sought throughout the story, gets the last word. But Flynn is a cold and heartless man. He has no solutions, only the doctrines of the Church.

Which was a damn sight more than I had, as I stumbled out of the crew van that hot June morning. I had missed breakfast, so I went straight to the snack table, which stood in the shade of the oak tree behind the O'Connor farmhouse. It was only seven o'clock, but slivers of intense sunlight already shot across the lawn, announcing another scorcher. I poured myself a black coffee and eavesdropped while the producer discussed the day's schedule with the assistant director, Terry Donnelly.

Having been racked by dry heaves half an hour earlier, I sipped my coffee carefully. Afraid to open my mouth too wide, I forced half a jelly doughnut past my teeth, sucked it back to my esophagus, then swallowed it in several gulps, the way a python ingests a rat. I wiped the sugar from my lips and fed the rest of the doughnut to one of the famous O'Connor peacocks that roamed the lawn. The day before, this same peacock had refused to show his startling tail to our cameras until I stood before him in my red-and-white-striped Greek soccer shirt and strutted about like a peacock myself. He and I were buddies now.

"Ready, Dusty?" asked Donnelly.

"Standing by," I said. I wanted to die. I would have given a week's salary to drop dead right there on the grass.

"Let's get to it then."

"You got it," I said, waiting for Donnelly to lead the way.

•  •  •

By the time I'd managed to maneuver the camera dolly into the tight quarters of the makeshift bedroom set, Lane Smith and Shirley Stoler were already in bed, running their lines. The two of them made a very convincing white trash couple — Lane with his dark, beady eyes and greasy undershirt; Shirley with . . . well, I'll get to that.

The non-insulated outbuilding that served as our set felt like an oven. We had blacked out the windows. A small fan turned meekly in the doorway, managing only to tease those of us who were squeezed into the narrow space on the opposite side of the bed. I could barely breathe.

Shirley's character, Mrs. Shortley, was trying to make sense of the threat the Pole presented to her way of life. Intuiting that even the Negroes might be replaced by a wave of European immigrants, she was articulating a newfound altruism to her half-asleep husband: "Chancey," she said, "turn thisaway. I hate to see niggers mistreated and run out. I have a heap of pity for niggers and poor folks. Ain't I always had? I say ain't I always been a friend to niggers and poor folks?"

Shirley's Southern accent seemed less than convincing, but she conveyed, without effort, the deep-seated treachery required of her character. There was about Shirley a natural aura of resentment, either caused by her constant physical discomfort or the cause of it — you couldn't tell which. Malice exuded from her pores on rivulets of sweat that the makeup woman daubed with tissues. The flesh on her arms was bubbly; the excess fat swallowed the elbow joints entirely. At her pinched wrists the skin had bruised to the color of storm clouds. Multiple chins overwhelmed her neck in waves, finally coming to rest on her chest. A mottled heat rash painted her cheeks. Her breasts rose and fell beneath her damp cotton shift as she panted in the stifling air. This was not just an overweight woman, but an actress who seemed to have coaxed her obesity from stone, invented it, nurtured it, honored it. In a previous film she had won accolades for playing a brutal Nazi prison camp commandant.

Now, as Shirley lay sprawled on the dingy sheets, waiting for Donnelly to quiet the set, her head rolled slowly and quite deliberately in my direction. Her gaze lingered on my crotch as she gave me the once-over, from sandals to headband. Her eyes narrowed. Then, smiling as pitilessly as she might have smiled at a mosquito, she locked her eyes on mine and winked.

The great thing about being a drunk is that you get to erase causal relationships. One event needn't be logically connected to the next. This allows you to muck about in the psychic depths and dredge up buckets of unambiguous — if inexplicable — terror. Heavy use of alcohol, nicotine, and cocaine exposes a person to raw experience, without the filters of reason and common sense.

Several days before Shirley winked at me, I woke abruptly from a hangover-induced Sunday nap, having dreamt that a lightning bolt struck the gold dome of a capitol somewhere. I had been unable to make sense of the dream, but in the immediate aftermath of Shirley's wink, I felt a residual electrical jolt. A normal man — one who allowed oxygen to aerate his blood — would probably have dealt with the wink with ease. In that gesture he might have sensed the kindness that actually did reside in Shirley's heart and responded naturally — maybe even winked back flirtatiously, thus defusing the situation — not, in any case, taking it personally, feeling a threat.

But I, in my dehydrated state, saw that wink as an unintelligible lightning bolt — a streak out of the unknown that suggested something I wasn't ready to consider: if Shirley so unabashedly desired me, then part of me must deserve that desire — match it, so to speak. But had I ever given this real-life woman any indication that I was interested in getting it on? Had I not made it clear every night in the local bar that the Georgia peaches who followed the crew around were more my style — and my just desserts? Had I not shown patience in my pursuit of these honeys, even though they showed far less interest in my scribbles than New York City girls did? Did my past conquests not shield me from assaults like this?

Apparently not. Like a man whose eyelids had been removed by torturers, I was compelled to stare at Shirley while she sized me up — all 150 pounds of me. I returned her come-on with a stony stare, disowning her wink utterly. But a film set is an unforgiving environment. People within it are aligned like iron filings in a magnetic field. When Shirley winked at me, she did so in a way that announced to everyone present not just her desire for me or her expectation of fulfillment, but a kind of done-dealness, suggesting that her desire for me had already been satisfied.

Donnelly did not ask for quiet on the set. He didn't have to. The eyes of my peers were upon me. Suddenly forced to try to recall where I had been and what I had done the previous night — before finding myself on the balcony — I blushed with all the fury of a schoolgirl.

"She wants you," whispered Lane. "She told me so this morning. She wants you bad."

"That's not even funny," I whispered back. But secretly I was elated to hear that nothing had transpired between Shirley and me, that I hadn't led her on, or worse, the night before, that it was all in her mind. "She's *your* wife, Mr. Shortley," I told the actor. "You're the one who's stuck with her. That's why you get the big bucks."

"Hah!" he said.

We were in the dairy barn, after lunch, preparing to film a scene in which Mr. Shortley asserts that he will not be intimidated by Father Flynn's plan to import more Polish workers. The sound man, Nigel Noble, asked Lane to read a line so he could get a decibel level. Lane cleared his throat and did so.

"Right, thank you," said Nigel, in his English accent. He took a nip from a fifth of Jack Daniel's he kept hidden on the sound cart, then offered me a hit. I took a gulp.

"Hey, Lane," I said, "read that line again."

Lane gave it his best drawl: "Ain't no Pope a Rome gonna tay-ell *me* how to run no day-ry."

We all laughed. The anxiety I had suffered since the bedroom scene was gone now. My gut felt warm. Beginning to feel a second wind, I found myself looking forward to the bar.

The prop man, Chris Kelly, led a Guernsey cow into the barn, struggling to get it in front of the camera. Having worked on a farm when I was a kid, I slapped the cow's rump, shoved it forward into the stanchion, secured the clasp, and returned to my own work. As I bent down to unlock the wheels of the camera dolly, someone slapped *my* rump, hard. I spun around, ready to clock whoever it was, and saw Shirley standing there (along with the makeup woman and producer), her fat hand held out to me. Reluctantly, I grasped her fingers and steadied her as she stepped across the dolly track. Thanking me, she curtsied and winked again.

I turned to Nigel. Already he was passing me the bottle.

"Icy blue" is the way Flannery O'Connor described Mrs. Shortley's eyes. Had I read her story at the time, I would have known that she had been tactful in her description of Mrs. Shortley's challenged body, and that she had, in fact, created an immensely sensitive portrait of a woman whose relationship to the unconscious was not unlike my own — dim, yet charged with receptivity. Mrs. Shortley had lightning-like visions. So did I. She maintained a constant proximity to death and a precarious relationship to the truth. So did I. She was crude, but no cruder than me. And she went about assuming that she was somebody she wasn't. So did I.

The differences between us were just as striking: I was not a fictional character in a story. Nor was I going to be allowed, as it turned out, to exit this life at a young age. And unlike Mrs. Shortley, I couldn't blame my shortcomings on my natal circumstances or on the region of America in which I was raised. I had a prep school and college education. I had been brought up by well-meaning, artistic parents, in an environment of unquestioned privilege in the Northeast. Whereas Mrs. Shortley wished constantly to rid herself of the social disgrace she perceived to be her lot, I was working like mad to achieve that disgrace.

What bridged the gap between our similarities and differences was the written (and unwritten) word. Flannery O'Connor had portrayed the dim-witted, uncomfortable-in-her-own-skin Mrs. Shortley not because she shared her bigoted sentiments but because those sentiments, when exposed, shed light on a deeper truth: that we are all in this together; that to love — to have it or give it — requires first an acknowledgment of shared humanity. O'Connor, knowing herself — and knowing her time was limited — shared her own humanity by writing about these things.

I, in portraying to those around me the dim-witted, uncomfortable-in-his-own-skin version of myself, was hardly that generous and brave. It would be years before I would quit drinking and begin to write. But I was, in my own way, chasing after — and held steady by — some deep need to share my lot in life with others. Beneath my drunken perversity ran a persistent and steady current: the knowledge that sooner or later I would have to account for myself — and that if all the pain I was going through were ever to prove worthwhile, I would have to put that account in writing. Already I was beginning to suspect that no amount of camaraderie at the bar was going to bring me closer to a shared humanity.

• • •

When Flannery O'Connor's mother, Regina Cline O'Connor, offered me iced tea on her front porch that afternoon, I nearly turned her down. The day before she had ordered all the men on the crew to put their shirts on while working anywhere near the house, despite the sweltering heat. Her dictum had caused widespread resentment, and being quick to take up futile causes, I had voiced my distaste for such manipulative and arbitrary Southern decorum.

But iced tea was iced tea, and I needed badly to sit on a rocker in the shade. I accepted the perspiring glass, doily and all, and looked through the screen at the view to the west. A gentle breeze carried the odor of rattlesnakes nesting in the nearby field. John Houseman, dressed as Father Flynn, and Irene Worth, made up as Mrs. McIntyre, sipped their tea on a white wicker couch nearby.

I remember that moment vividly, perhaps because it played out in silence, since I didn't know enough to recognize this privilege, this opportunity. I didn't ask, "Mrs. O'Connor, did Flannery sit on this rocker in the days before she died? Was it hard on her to be so deathly ill and still feel compelled to write? Did writing help to shield her from a fear of death?" And I didn't declare, "Your daughter is my mother's favorite writer." Or "When I was still a boy, Flannery was living up north and writing stories a few miles from where my family lived. We swam in the same lake."

I didn't last in the bar that night. It seemed I was invisible to the Southern belles, and I just didn't have the energy to get my tail all afluff. I ate steak and drank four or five fingers of bourbon from a beer mug filled with ice, then caught a ride back to the motel with Lane and his driver.

Feeling proud of myself for having pulled the plug before midnight, I took a long shower, arranged my clothes for the morning, then lay down on the bed and turned out the light. Lying there in the dark, I remembered how the day had begun. I forced myself to get up and unlock the motel room door, just in case I found myself out there in front of the populace again.

Lying back down, naked atop the fresh sheets, I fell asleep in the cool of the air-conditioned room. I am not sure exactly what woke me an hour later, but it was probably the sound of a raspy breath not my own — or the strange weight drawing me into the center of the bed. I opened my eyes. There lay Shirley, mountainous beside me, her hand reaching out to stroke my face.

# 6

# Leaving the Garden

I NEVER PLANNED a career in the film business. I loved movies but had no particular urge to work on them. At age thirty-one, I had a wife and two children. My one-year-old son suffered from a serious and inoperable heart condition. To make ends meet, I'd been driving a New York City taxicab and picking up a few bucks on the side with freelance photography. After I volunteered to help a friend who was shooting the tag end of a low-budget feature, word soon got around that I was a hard worker. Producers started employing me as a kind of all-purpose crew member.

The first full-length feature film I ever worked on was a low-budget Merchant Ivory production called *Savages,* starring Sam Waterston and Susie Blakely, which began shooting in the summer of 1971.

*Savages* begins with a series of intertitled black-and-white sequences purporting to show the activities of a Stone Age forest tribe called the Mud People. One day at dawn, these masked and mud-covered savages prepare for their annual human sacrifice by feeding a powerful narcotic leaf to the consort of their queen. Just as the sacrifice is about to be carried out, a small spherical object comes sailing over the treetops and lands on the forest floor. Naturally the queen of the tribe sees great significance in this. The Mud People abandon their sacrifice and follow the mysteriously rolling object — a croquet ball, as it turns out — through the woods, until it leads them to a huge colonial mansion in a tidy clearing. The tribe cautiously enters the mansion, led by its youngest member, a girl. You can see wonder in the girl's eyes as she takes in the wide central staircase and the huge chandelier, and you can imagine her thinking, *Wow! This is a happening place!*

The Mud People explore the lavishly furnished but inexplicably abandoned rooms of the mansion. One of the women discovers an oil portrait of a preppy-looking boy and licks his face; another tries on an evening gown and learns how to use scissors. The queen herself places the croquet ball at the base of a statue of a naked woman, thus creating an altar. One of the men figures out the purpose of a pair of spectacles and puts them on. Predictably, the savages are seduced by the material comforts they find in the mansion. As they remove their primitive masks and wash off the mud, they are transformed into recognizable early-twentieth-century stereotypes — a songwriter, a capitalist, a hostess, a debutante, and so on.

When I first arrived at Beechwood Mansion in upstate New York to begin work on *Savages,* I was pretty much following my own personal croquet ball. Like the Mud People, I was propelled more by curiosity than ambition. Compared to the social upheaval of the 1970s — exploding racial tensions, widespread alcohol and drug use, rampant sexual experimentation — domestic life simply paled. Working on a feature film — away from home, away from the reality of my son's illness — offered a welcome diversion. The pay stank — $150 a week, flat — but it was enough to keep my family going in a two-bedroom apartment on Manhattan's Upper West Side.

That first day at the mansion, just as dawn was breaking, our three-man crew unloaded a standard package of lighting and grip equipment and staged everything in the house. My immediate boss was the gaffer, a fellow who called himself Bobby V. Bobby, who had done jail time in Chicago for burglary and car theft, looked like Ichabod Crane — tall, gaunt, and intimidating. He was nervous on this day because his own boss was none other than Walter Lassally, a British cinematographer who had recently won an Academy Award for his work on *Zorba the Greek*.

I kept my mouth shut and proceeded to lay out long lines of electrical feeder cable, dropping the coils at the generator and dragging one end across the lawn and into the mansion. At 7 A.M., everyone else showed up. The cast disappeared immediately into the wardrobe room right off the main lobby. I helped the best boy electrician set up the tungsten lights on rolling stands. I scurried around connecting extension cables to the light heads and plugging the extensions into the stage distribution boxes located in the hallways. Soaked with sweat and streaked with dirt, I taped up all the connections, while James Ivory, Ismail Merchant, and Walter Lassally floated around effortlessly in leather sandals and clean linen clothing, making artistic decisions. I had always thought of myself as a creative person, but I relished this physical labor. Here was a job — unlike the novel writing I was trying to do — that had a substantial shape to it. Compared to facing a blank sheet of paper in my typewriter, the task of setting up film equipment was a huge relief.

None of us had seen the film script, written by George W. S. Trow. And I for one had no idea what the movie was about. That it might be an allegory mattered as little to me as the broader purpose of a war matters to a soldier on his first day in combat. Since I was a lackey at heart, it was enough for me that the actors had stellar theatrical reputations — people like Lewis J. Stadlen, Thayer David, Salome Jens, and Kathleen Widdoes. And of course there was Susie Blakely, who today would be called a supermodel; Ultra Violet, a veteran actress in Andy Warhol's films; and Sam Waterston.

When the cast made their first grand appearance on the set, I happened to be on my knees, struggling to jam a bent stage plug into one of the distribution boxes. Blue-and-white sparks flew from the box every time I tried to insert the thing. Half-blinded by arcing flashes of electricity, I looked up and saw the entire cast fanning out from the dressing room door into the wide entranceway of the mansion — all sixteen of them, ranging in age from fourteen to eighty, stark naked except for their mud masks and, in a few cases, loincloths. My jaw dropped.

Just then Susie Blakely, wearing neither loincloth nor mask, approached me with two dripping gobs of gray mud, one in each hand. She looked for all the world like the biblical Eve bearing an offering of two apples. She stopped and stood in front of me — me, on my knees like some supplicant beggar — smiled her all-American smile, and said, "There aren't enough makeup people. Would you mind rubbing this mud on me?"

My first thought was that I had electrocuted myself. It was a writerly kind of thought, and as such, was slow and ponderous to emerge. In the several seconds it took me to think it, Bobby V. swooped in, grabbed both gobs of mud from Susie's hands, and announced, "*I'll* take care of this."

Susie, clearly sensing my disappointment, transferred what little mud was left from her hands to mine, which were absurdly outstretched in her direction. "You can do my ankles," she said.

And I did. I settled for Susie's ankles.

Some experiences in life, when we look back at them, seem to contain the seeds of everything that follows. No matter how

long we go on kissing the one we love, it is the first kiss we remember. So too, no matter how many days we show up to per-
form the work we decide to do, we are basically refining and
polishing the original thing — the prototypical experience. In
this way the shape of a whole career can be divined from a single moment of work. My lackey position in the hierarchy of the
film business was set in stone when I agreed, that day, to remain
on my knees, massaging mud onto the ankles of a naked fashion
model, a woman who — like Eve — personified lost innocence.

We shot the black-and-white scenes first. The second act, which
we shot in color, began with a dreamy sequence titled IN THE
SCHOOLYARD, which opened with the beautiful and scantily
clad Salome Jens swinging happily on a huge outdoor swing.
The allegorical implication was clear: many of the impulses that
led to what we call civilization — like many of the impulses that
led me to a career in the film business — were childlike, playful,
and pure. There was a time, the movie seems to suggest, when
wonderment and gaiety and joyous participation outweighed the
forces of cynicism, morbidity, and socially sanctioned greed.

The first week's work on *Savages* exemplified such a time.
The more responsibility they dumped on me, the more eager I
was to work. In addition to my duties helping the electrician, I
was given the position of dolly grip, which meant that I worked
directly with Walter Lassally whenever the camera moved during the filming of a scene. It also meant that I had to work twice
as hard for the same amount of money. But no one — not even
Walter — was getting paid very much. This infused us all with
a wonderful no-strings-attached, egalitarian spirit — both during and after work. That I was a sweat-covered neophyte did not
prevent Sam Waterston from sharing a joint with me when the
day was done. That Kathy Widdoes was an experienced actress
did not deter her from asking my opinion of her performance.

The harder we worked in those first days, the more intimate

the cast and crew became. I began to aggressively seek the company of Kathy and Ultra and Susie and Salome — sometimes all four of them at once — and I very quickly began to envision a more exotic social life than that of a wannabe writer and financially strapped family man. To sustain this fantasy, I happily added four hours of intense partying to my sixteen-hour workday.

But since a more exotic life was not really available to me — I mean, nothing in my life had *actually* changed — the fantasy soon became exhausting. I was not alone in this exhaustion. No one likes to be overworked and underpaid — not even actors, who stand to achieve immortality in the bargain. After about a week, the wonderment of selfless community and egalitarian good times finally gave way to cynicism, morbidity, and greed. Needing — all of us — to position ourselves professionally for the long haul, the cast retreated into its shell of creative superiority, and the crew into servitude.

The schoolyard sequence of *Savages* ends when the newly sophisticated savages discover a dead wolfhound lying on the steps of the garden. They don't know what to make of the dog's death. But we do. It is the death of egalitarianism. Equality is not enough for the human spirit. Neither is innocence or gaiety. In the background of the dead wolfhound scene — in the dusk — the lights of the mansion blink on and off, beckoning the new sophisticates to the next sequence, announced by a title card that reads THE DINNER PARTY.

It has been said that working on a movie is like being in combat, with its long periods of waiting and its sudden bursts of urgent activity. But it is also very much like attending a cocktail or dinner party. Imagine, if you can, being face to face in tight quarters with the same fifty people, sixteen hours a day, six days a week. Movie stars and principal actors are allowed to retire to dressing rooms and trailers. But everyone else on the set must be prepared to *relate* at all times. This requires maintaining a persona throughout the day, and to do this, you need the appropriate constructs: a solid self-image of some kind and a recognizable position in the hierarchy of the company. To get a seat at the dinner table, you must demonstrate some kind of authority.

On *Savages* I had felt perfectly content, at first, to be whatever anyone wanted me to be — electrician, grip, gofer, I didn't care — as long as everyone else was willing to do likewise. But I soon learned that if I wanted to maintain my distance from the domestic scene and prolong my avoidance of writing — and I felt an urgent need to do both — I would need to define myself in some recognizable way. As it happened, I had a natural instinct for rigging, and Walter Lassally loved my dolly moves. So I began to flirt with the idea of becoming a key grip.

A key grip supervises the rigging of all the lights — on ceiling grids, construction cranes, scaffolding, and so on — and all the subtle diffusion of light, both artificial and natural. Grips are responsible for the construction and placement of set walls, as well as for all the dolly shots, car rigging, stunt preparations, set safety, and so on. The key grip is the chief problem solver on a movie set, and as such needs to be able to analyze things quickly and make snap decisions in matters that affect many other departments — and often a great deal of the producer's money. People always need a key grip's advice. If you are a timid writer who has lost all hope of a readership, become a key grip. It will change your life. Famous directors and cameramen will ask for your opinion — will this or that shot work? Movie stars, knowing that your concern for their safety is an integral part of their immortality, will address you by name and ask if you slept well the night before.

I remember one job — a Jell-O commercial — for which I had to drive a large camera crane, quite fast, right up to Bill Cosby's face, take after take after take. Cosby, who can be very curt to people who work with him, spent half the day following me around and making small talk in order to ensure that he remained on my good side. Bill and I were the best of buddies.

Notice that I have dropped a celebrity name. Without the reference to famous directors, and the inclusion of Bill Cosby's name, my job description would read like a help-wanted notice tacked on a bulletin board at a construction site. This raises the very real possibility that if the movie set of *Savages* had in fact been an everyday construction site, I probably would have concluded that the brutal hours and low pay were exploitative and cruel, and I might well have retreated into writerly anonymity —free then to examine my soul and produce volumes of creative work.

But this phenomenon of fame by association is a powerful and seductive drug. It loves a creative void. Freud would probably liken it to libido. I liken it to static cling. Once you have experienced it (people describe heroin this way), the bar is set for life.

Over the years, I worked on the early films of actors such as Susan Sarandon, Jeff Goldblum, Michael Moriarty, Paul Sorvino, Treat Williams, Samuel L. Jackson, John Heard, Tim Robbins, John Turturro, Raul Julia, Margaux Hemingway, Rick Belzer, Chevy Chase, and Matt Damon and his buddy Ben Affleck, to name a few. If pressed, I will gladly call attention to my having rubbed elbows with iconic figures like Robert De Niro, Martin Scorcese, Charlton Heston, Sylvester Stallone, Spike Lee, Irene Worth, Anjelica Huston, Mick Jagger, Ice-T, Elliot Gould, Woody Allen, Warren Beatty, Gene Hackman, Carly Simon, Raquel Welch, Catherine Deneuve, Marcello Mastroianni, Chuck Yeager, various Apollo astronauts, Henry Kissinger, several U.S. presidents, Pope John Paul II, and oh yes, the supermodel Elle Macpherson.

If one of these celebrity names comes up in casual conversation, I usually cannot resist mentioning that I "worked with" him or her or that I "did" his or her film. Dropping a celebrity name makes me feel better about myself.

I did not return to writerly anonymity when we finished shooting *Savages.* I began billing myself as a key grip, even though I had never even met a real key grip. There is some precedent for this kind of moxie. I once asked a Native American medicine man what you had to do to become a medicine man. "The first step," he said, "is to call yourself one." By referring to myself as a key grip, I made a place for myself at the dinner table. Like one of the sophisticated savages, I could now walk the walk and talk the talk. And my brand of medicine seemed to work. Producers like to see confidence in their department heads, and I exuded confidence. I wore a red kerchief around my neck and sported a large bowie knife on my belt; at one point I even wore a cowboy hat. If, during a job interview, the producer questioned my experience, I would simply distract him or her with a reference to, say, Kierkegaard or Camus. This would nearly always leave a producer blinking.

I joined a young film union to make my job title official. The pay got considerably better. I bought a small truck and stocked it with specialized rigging and grip equipment. In partnership with a cameraman, I started a film equipment rental company called Feature Systems. It was exhilarating. For every film I accepted, I turned down five. And between films, I worked on hundreds of commercials, where the real money was.

In the early 1970s, when competent film crews could be found only in Los Angeles or New York, we traveled all over the country to make movies and commercials. We invaded and occupied small towns, wowing the women, ravaging the supplies of liquor and beer, hiring local police forces as our security personnel. We turned paved roads into dirt and paved over dirt roads; we built false-front façades on main streets, then tore them down. We transformed spring into autumn and summer into winter, caused rainstorms and produced lightning. Then when we had had our way with a place — when we had infused it with static cling — we would pull out in a cloud of diesel exhaust, leaving behind piles of used lumber and stacks of broken hearts, the way traveling circuses used to do.

During the dinner party sequence of *Savages*, the former Mud People dress up in tuxedoes and evening gowns, gather at a long table, and spend a large part of the evening posturing and dropping names. The relationships among the guests are discernible only in terms of the power one person exerts — or does not exert — over another. Innuendo rules the conversation. Subtle and not-so-subtle insults are hurled, and grand pomposities articulated.

When the women retire to the library, the men light up cigars, and Sam Waterston's character tells a story about a mysterious Stone Age tribe called the Mud People. His intellectual affectation prevents him from remembering that he and his fellow sophisticates were, only twelve hours ago, Mud People themselves.

When we cut to the women having coffee in the library, Ultra Violet tells Salome Jens that one of the older men at the table seemed to be a very powerful person.

"Otto is a bluffer," replies Salome. "We are none of us very powerful here."

"But he's treated with respect by our hostess," says Ultra. "He's deferred to."

At this point Salome leans toward Ultra and delivers one of the key lines in the film: "You do know," she says, "it is all going on somewhere else."

"What is?" asks Ultra.

"Everything," says Salome.

And there it is. For all the hullabaloo and dinner-party atmosphere of filmmaking, the lived lives of the participants happen somewhere else. As hard as I tried to mask the inevitable with newfound ambition, hard work, and a film biz moniker, my son died four months after *Savages* wrapped. My daughter was six at the time. Her mother and I got an amicable divorce the following year. For a decade, I embraced drugs and alcohol and promiscuity and dabbled in the occult. I gave up my equipment company and traveled to Chichén Itzá to sit on a pyramid. In the early 1980s, after quitting drugs, alcohol, and cigarettes, I got married again, this time to a woman who was also in the business. We bought a house in the country and one hundred acres of land, and planned to have a child together. I spent my weekends mowing the lawn and raking leaves and shoveling snow. My daughter graduated from high school. Between film jobs I started to write again. I completed a novel about a film producer. It was judged by publishers to be quite well written but ultimately disappointing — perhaps because I had never been a film producer myself. My daughter graduated from college. I got divorced again. My parents died. Then one day I looked at the movie set, and suddenly everyone seemed terribly young.

I do not mean to suggest that working around movie stars was devoid of life and familiarity. I shared genuine moments of casual intimacy with certain of the celebrities I have mentioned. At the very least I retain snippets of memory about each of them — tidbits that have survived my twenty-seven-year stint in the business. Some of these memories seem almost surreal now, like the time Bobby V. and I, in the company of Treat Williams and his girlfriend, snorted cocaine from a tablecloth in one of New York's famous four-star restaurants, while the headwaiter and patrons looked on, mesmerized and appalled.

Or this:

It is the first day of shooting on the movie *Cop Land*. From my position behind the dolly, I am trying to size up Sylvester Stallone, who is standing a few feet away. His muscular back and ropy shoulders suggest a well-developed shell. His posture exudes rigidity. His reptilian eyelids veil surprisingly sad eyes. How much of this is Stallone, and how much is Freddy, the character he is playing, is hard to tell. In any case, I am secretly hoping for some eye contact — something to break the ice — since, after all, we will be working in close proximity for the next two months. Basically I am gawking, of course, just like one of the many spectators held at bay behind the police barricades. Suddenly Stallone's eyes sweep my way, too fast for me to affect professional disinterest. But I needn't worry; his gaze passes over me like an unmanned beacon in a prison yard. The effect is chilling.

Just then, the young director, James Mangold, approaches Stallone and asks him to tone down the sadness he had been projecting earlier during rehearsals. "Remember, Sly, you aren't really depressed yet, at this point in the script. What you really are at this point is . . ." — and here Mangold pauses for effect — ". . . what you're really feeling right now is . . . *lugubrious*."

"Lugubrious?" asks Stallone.

Our eyes never do meet — Stallone's and mine — even on the smallest of sets. But from that day on, in every on-set interview he gives to the media, I hear him interject his newfound bit of vocabulary: *lugubrious*. Perhaps because of this, I actually like him.

Or, at the warm end of the intimacy spectrum, take the movie *Compromising Positions,* starring Susan Sarandon and Raul Julia: It is a fine summer day in East Hampton, New York, 1984. Susan is sitting in the driver's seat of a car rigged with lights and cameras and diffusion frames. My crew is attaching the car to the tow vehicle, getting us ready to head out on back roads for a running shot. I knock on the driver's-side window to give Susan instructions about what not to do while we are on the road — don't use the brakes, let the car steer itself — but for some reason Susan moves over and beckons me to sit down next to her. I open the door, slide in beside her, and close the door behind me. The commotion outside suddenly sounds far away. Some of the guys take their tools and move away from the car. Susan sidles closer to me, hooks her arm in mine, then rests her head on my shoulder. She is four months pregnant with her first child and has decided not to marry the child's father. My second wife has recently discovered she cannot have children. Susan and I know these things about each other, but neither of us says a word. My left hand clutches the steering wheel, my right foot presses the gas pedal. For one long hallucinatory moment, we drive off into the sunset together.

As the dinner party sequence of *Savages* ends, a strange new title, written in classical Greek, comes at us from the depths of the dark screen and sparkles for several seconds before it disappears: OLESI-KARPOS. *Olesi* means "to destroy." *Karpos* means "fruit." *Karpos* is not just any kind of fruit; it is the bounty the ancient Greeks offered to the gods — the sacrifice. The phrase *olesi-karpos* shows up in the tenth book of Homer's *Odyssey*, where Circe tells Odysseus that if he wants to enter Hades and survive to tell the tale, he must first make a sacrifice. She instructs him to make that sacrifice when he comes to a place where tall poplars and "fruit-destroying" willows grow.

The connotative meaning of the term *olesi-karpos*, the one that applies to our savages — and to me — is this: they drop their unripe fruit, they squander their substance. Distracted first by the croquet ball and then by their new lifestyle, the savages completely forget to offer up their sacrifice. As a result they throw away their potential as civilized human beings. Having lost touch with anything more important than their own affect, they find themselves adrift. Which is why everything seems to them to be happening someplace else.

Following the dinner party, the hostess, Carlotta (the queen of the tribe), gathers everyone in the library and reads the future from an overripe piece of fruit — the *karpos*. As if peering into a crystal ball, Carlotta intones her dark vision of the future with words like *duplicity, abasement, remorse, obscurity*. Her fellow sophisticates listen raptly, but they have no clue as to what her prophecy means. Susie Blakely's character simply giggles. If the notion of a neglected sacrifice occurs to anyone, it is only subliminally. They drift away and play records on a wind-up Victrola. The Lewis J. Stadlen character — the songwriter — performs one of his new compositions. Carlotta judges the songwriter's work to be — like my novel — quite well performed but ultimately disappointing. The group disperses and everyone goes outside to have drinks around the swimming pool. Everyone, that is, except the songwriter — who, after his failure in the hoopla world of the mansion, absents himself from all the hype, choosing instead to play his cello — alone — in the night-shrouded solarium.

After that everything begins to fall apart for the others. Sam Waterston's character drowns himself in the pool, intentionally and in front of everyone. No one stops him, which makes his death a perverse and unconscious sacrifice. His girlfriend is found hanging by her neck from the limb of a tree, another botched sacrifice.

In the wee hours of the morning, the sophisticates join together in a round of yogic chanting and partake of a powdered drug. Then they file down into the basement (Hades), where they engage in ritual exhibitionist behavior and game playing. They rediscover the ancient symbol of the spiral, as things continue to spiral downward. They fight over possessions and bright jewels. They humiliate and degrade one another and squabble over the carcass of a chicken.

When dawn finally comes, the now *un*sophisticated savages rush up from the basement (from their own abasement) and, after smashing all the Victrola records (the records of civilization), run out onto the lawn to play a rowdy game of croquet. They smack the balls into the pasture and, in a spirit of wild abandon, follow the rolling balls back into the forest — presumably back to their Stone Age lifestyle. There, we imagine, they will forget about their experience with civilization and pick up where they left off with their primitive sacrifice, which consists of crushing the skull of the queen's consort with a huge rock.

Only one of the savages lingers at the mansion: the songwriter. Or, let us say, the writer. Before running off into the forest, the writer watches bemusedly as his fellow savages flee the experience of civilization, and he takes a moment to ponder what that experience might mean.

After thirty-odd years I am struck by Susie Blakeley's almost biblical offering to me. Looking back on it now, I see her enticement — two gobs of gray mud — as a vision of alternative possibilities, the mud of creation, the mud of the grave. Write or die.

I sometimes marvel that I spent the prime of my life in a servile relationship to an art not my own. I can never get that time back. What was I doing there all of those years?

Recently I called the gaffer Bobby V., whom I had not seen for years. I guess certain statutes of limitation have run out, because he goes by his real name now, Robert Vercruse. He lives with his wife in the country and works only occasionally on films. I asked him why, thirty-three years ago, he had made the seemingly fantastical leap from a career as a cat burglar and car thief in Chicago to working as a gaffer on movies in New York.

"That's easy," he said. "The adrenaline rush of working on movies was better than stealing."

I would take it one step further: working on movies *was* stealing. Under the cover of servitude, I pilfered the sensation of celebrity; appropriated by association the identities of the famous; embezzled the ambition of the powerful; borrowed funereal episodes of despair and grief; pinched moments of hysterical laughter and promise; lifted for weeks at a time the lifestyles of the rich; hijacked the desperate environment of the poor; pocketed plots and structure; and made off with meaning and arc. It was all about story, all along. The sacrifice — the offering up of story —that comes at the end.

# 7

# When You Finish Your Beer

Y OU'RE TWENTY-SEVEN years old, and you don't have
a clue yet, do you? No idea what you're really seeing
across the street. Just a tall black man, standing alone
and motionless in the center of the sidewalk, wearing a red bandanna. You're sitting sideways in an open window five floors up,
sipping Miller beer from a frosted mug. The evening ushers in
a welcome breeze. Your wife is reading to your daughter in another room: *Petunia,* the goose. Sounds drift up from the block:
bongo drums, the clack of dominoes on a tabletop. Staccato
chatter, followed by hoarse laughter. From a transistor radio
you can hear staticky bursts of news in Spanish — something or
other about the progress of the war in Vietnam and President
Johnson's latest assessment. A reference to Martin Luther King
Jr. You light a Marlboro, the last in the pack you opened this
morning. You chase the hot smoke with beer, lean out, and spit.
The man with the red bandanna hasn't moved an inch. He's staring at a crack in the sidewalk, puzzled by what he sees.

You like this perch. It provides you with a God-like omniscience. You like to think you've developed the eyes of a hawk, but you keep an old pair of binoculars on a nearby hook, just in case. A week ago you saw a man shot down there, a middle-aged guy dressed in a khaki trench coat and lugging a tan briefcase home from work, making his way toward Riverside Drive. He took a bullet right between the eyes, fell face first, hit the pavement like a parade-ground soldier. You never heard the shot ("not even a pop," you told a detective later). But you saw the man's hand fly open and the briefcase drop. An hour later, they found the kid who did it. He was sitting on his mother's bed, engrossed in a comic book, a .22-caliber rifle on his lap.

Eighty-fifth Street is littered with subject matter. Take Renaldo, for instance, the pimp who lives across the street, a few buildings west. Lean out a little farther and you can see him, hair all slicked up like Little Richard's, sitting just inside that first-floor window, looking out from the darkness of his room. One elbow rests on a purple cushion he keeps on his windowsill. He's staring at his new cream-colored Caddy, with its two circular side windows and its sky blue dashboard rug. Soon he'll be out and about in a white suit and a broad-brimmed chartreuse hat, everyone around him cowed by his flamboyance. The rumor is that he has three whores.

What's up with Bandanna Man? He's bracing himself for big things now. Totally zoned out on heroin, still staring in disbelief at the crack in the sidewalk: a chasm. He's tilting back a little on his heels, and his hands are raised, as if he's about to make a passionate declaration of despair. What is his problem?

You put down your beer, take the binoculars off the hook, and focus them on the pavement in front of him. There's the problem, wedged in the crack: a bright wooden matchstick, its self-strike phosphorus tip still intact. You pan the glasses to the right. Bony knees, slightly bent, the right one poking through a rip in the man's pitiful jeans. Scuffed black shoes, the left with-

out a lace. No socks. Fly wide open. What a wreck. You'll jot
down those details when you finish your beer, you tell yourself.

You're going to fail, aren't you? That's still to come. Put the
binoculars back on the hook. Don't let your beer get warm. No
way you can know it yet, but for all your bright ambition, you'll
wind up, four years from now, renting a little two-room dump
at the other end of this block — without your wife and kid. No
way to predict how many seasons, how many years in a row
you'll stumble home from the bar after work, beneath this very
window. Do you already sense the attraction — the raw mag-
netism — of the dissipated life? Do you really want to knuckle
down and write? What do you imagine for yourself as a consequence? Success? Be honest. Is it love?

There's this quart of beer to finish up, right here next to you
on the sill. And a spare bottle in the fridge for later. Be careful
not to drop the mug out the window. Wouldn't want to distract
Bandanna Man. Look how he's got his left foot lifted six inches
off the ground, like a stork in shallow water looking for a fish.
His hands, waist-high, move slowly sideways, for balance. Fingers stretched like a hurdler's, to the limit. Just about to take
that giant step.

You still don't get it do you? There's you up here, and then
there's him down there. Oh, you'll manage aphorisms on napkins
at the bar, and the rumor of your opus will precede you into every
room. The empty page. Your unstruck match.

# 8

# Jump

---

O N   A   F I N E   M A Y   M O R N I N G   in 1963, a parachuting buddy stopped by my apartment on New York
City's Upper West Side. Jim was the reigning world
champion skydiver. His handsome likeness had been captured
recently on the Camel cigarettes sign in Times Square. He'd
rented a tiny room right around the corner from the famous ad,
so he could just step out there on Broadway, beer in hand, and
admire those giant smoke rings wobbling from the steam pipe
hidden in his billboard lips.

"That's me," he'd tell passersby.

I was grateful that Jim had seen fit to tear himself away from
himself long enough to visit me. I was an undergraduate at Columbia University and had moved on from skydiving, but the
sport still had its hook in me. We cooked up a pound of bacon
and a ton of eggs and were recounting our most riveting parachuting stories when we heard yelling outside. "Call the police!
Call the police! She's going to jump!"

On the sidewalk, a middle-aged man wearing a khaki overcoat was pointing straight up. "Stop her!" he shouted, stamping the pavement. "She's going to jump!" Four floors above him — directly across from us — a dark-haired young woman stood barefoot on a narrow balcony. As I tried to make sense of the scene, she jumped.

I don't mean that she simply stepped over the knee-high railing and leapt into midair. Rather, she left the balcony in precisely the fashion I would have taught a beginner to jump from a single-engine Cessna. Taking hold of the railing, as if it were the wing strut of an airplane, she stepped calmly onto the ledge and turned her back on the middle-aged man below. She held this crouched position for a moment, hesitating, as any student jumper would, then kicked her feet out directly behind her and pushed off with both hands.

Jim was halfway downstairs before the woman actually jumped. I doubt he had time to notice that she wore a dark blouse, only partially buttoned in front, and black chino pants that seemed, before she hit, too tight around the waist. It was later rumored that she and the middle-aged man had been lovers. Someone suggested he was her professor. Safe to assume that there had been a crucial error at the heart of their relationship. Whatever imbalance that error had triggered, she wound up harnessing gravity to even the scales, though nothing in her calm demeanor had suggested that she actually intended to harm herself — or him. In any case, she could not have been thinking lucidly. Who would jump, even from a city stoop, in bare feet?

I'd always taught first-time jumpers to keep their eyes on me as they fell away from the plane. "Maintain a head-high position before the chute opens," I would tell them. "If you look down, you'll nose down." Well, this woman, this jumper, looked down. Had she begun counting up from *one thousand one* when she left the balcony, she would have gotten no further than *one thousand two* before she hit. Hardly enough time to gasp. She landed on the crown of her head in the center of the sidewalk.

I must have blinked just at that moment. My memory of the impact consists of only the sound — harsher by far than the crack of a rifle or the slap of an ax against oak. Was I, even then, racking my brain for words, for the aural equivalent of the popping open of a human skull? If so, my efforts were derailed by the inhuman howl that issued from the middle-aged man. A pool of thick blood widened around his black shoes.

The building superintendent, who must have been standing at the front door all along, suddenly yanked a blue kerchief from his back pocket and began to polish the brass doorknob — a touch too vigorously. On the balcony above, a pigeon cocked its head this way and that, as if puzzled by the woman's failed flight.

Jim and a few other onlookers watched from a distance, but no larger crowd gathered. Neighbors didn't shout the news to one another, as they would six months later, the day of President Kennedy's assassination. The woman's body was removed by ambulance and the middle-aged man went off in a squad car. The superintendent hosed the blood from the sidewalk, deftly adjusting the spray as he channeled first red, then pink, then clear water into the gutter drain. When the pavement dried, he hosed it down again.

# 9

# Grace

I F YOUR PARACHUTE doesn't open, you'll hit the ground at 125 miles per hour. This means going from a vertical speed of 174 feet per second to a dead stop, instantly. The resulting energy (mass times acceleration) splinters bone and liquefies cartilage, and usually shoots the innards, if not through a ruptured abdominal wall, then directly out the anus. You might bounce, you might not. But to the folks who will have to convey you from the scene, your body will feel rubbery and limp, like a jump suit stuffed with applesauce and gristle.

I knew the risk, on that moonless March night in 1960, as I sat crammed behind the pilot, waiting to make my 152nd jump. It was the kind of stuff we instructors joked about every night in bars, when our students weren't around. *Creaming in,* we called it, and *buying the farm.* I know now that I was risking my life. But if you'd asked me back then what risking my life meant, I'd have deflected the question with a cocky grin. At the age of nineteen, my notion of the future remained as opaque and featureless as the California desert a mile and a half below.

. . .

We'd taken off just after dusk from a nearby dirt airstrip, in a four-place Cessna 180. The aircraft, its right door and passenger seat removed, had been climbing steadily for twenty minutes. The whine of the Lycoming engine, combined with the staccato *whap-whap-whap* of the propeller, made casual conversation inside the cabin impossible. Hot exhaust swirled about in the turbulent air, its oily stink mixing with the odor of old upholstery and adding to the tension in my bowels.

The last rays of sunlight had long since abandoned the high cirrus clouds, leaving night to settle on the horizon. From my back-seat window, I could just make out the lights of San Diego, eighty miles to the west, and I found myself staring at the city's glow the way a child might gaze at the sliver of light beneath a bedroom door. God knows, looking straight down into the darkness brought little comfort. From that altitude, our intended target, a white canvas cross lit by two sets of car headlights, looked like a life raft floating on an ocean of ink.

This was my first free fall at night, and the onset of darkess made me more aware of my usual pre-jump jitters. Increased vertigo; anxiety about dropping my flashlight in free fall; fear of collision with another jumper in the dark. I intended to jot down these observations later. As the plane continued to climb, I wondered how Hemingway would treat the material. *Men waiting to jump.* That was the gist of it. It just begged for the kind of brief, declarative sentences that could rocket a writer to immortality. *Men waiting to jump . . .*

Bill Jolly, a veteran skydiver in his late thirties, sat on the floor next to the pilot, his back against the instrument panel. As I studied his rugged, impassive face for some sign that he shared my apprehension, he stifled a yawn with his hand. *There it is,* I thought. *Men waiting to jump always yawn.* No, that wasn't it. *Confronted with the jaws of death, men always yawn.* No. *A yawn is to a skydiver what spit is to a batter at the plate . . .*

By this time, I was yawning. So was Jimmy Lynn, the thirty-year-old, 275-pound karate expert who sat next to me on the back seat. Nerves. Little was known then about the behavior of the human body falling at terminal velocity, and even less about "relative work" — two or more bodies in free fall together.

Understand that the free-fall part of a parachute jump takes place between the exit altitude (in this case, seventy-five hundred feet) and the recommended opening altitude (twenty-five hundred feet). On this particular night, we planned to free fall for one mile — thirty seconds — before opening our chutes. (Follow the sweep hand on a watch, if you need help imagining it.)

The plane banked steeply, then leveled onto jump run. Jimmy Lynn, getting a nod from the pilot, slid forward on the seat and stuck his helmeted head out the door. His chin strap flapped wildly, and his bubble goggles shuddered atop his nose. Using the bottom edge of the doorway as a sighting device, he peered straight down.

"Where are we?" he called out to the pilot. "I can't see shit down there!"

"Should be coming up on the target!" answered the pilot.

Lynn looked again, then raised his hand. "Got it! Jesus fucking Christ! Do you think they could have made it a little smaller?"

I tapped the glass on my altimeter, checking that the needle wasn't stuck. The bulky instrument was strapped to my chest-mounted reserve chute and would be my only means of knowing when to pull the ripcord. I tested my flashlight — essential for reading the altimeter — then tightened the chin strap on my Bell helmet. My fingers trembled — something I hoped Jolly wouldn't notice.

"Right ten!" yelled Lynn.

The pilot kicked right rudder, making a flat correction of ten degrees.

"Ten more! Ten more!"

Again the plane jerked right.

Lynn was screaming now. "No! Twenty! Twenty! Twenty!"

The pilot glanced over his shoulder, eyeballing me and smirking. I swatted his arm in response, which made him laugh. I welcomed his levity, wished it would spread. You had to laugh. *Men waiting to jump must laugh.*

Bill Jolly wasn't laughing. Indeed, he looked quite uneasy. Maneuvering to a kneeling position on the floor, he switched on his flashlight, then signaled me to do the same. I nodded, giving him a thumbs-up and winking. Still, his anxiety had unsettled me. I checked that my ripcord handle was secure in its elastic housing, then fingered the pins on the reserve chute to be sure they were seated. I tested the Capewell releases that connected the parachute to the harness, and felt the snap connectors on my leg straps. Everything was set. I'd done all I could. There was only the jumping now. I took a deep breath. We'd be in the bar in an hour, I told myself. Indulging in raucous laughter, scoring chicks.

"Ten more!" Lynn clutched his flashlight close to his body.

Were we that far off course? I wanted to see for myself, but Lynn's enormous bulk prevented it. Stuck in the corner and squirming to get some leg room, I set my flashlight on the seat behind him and tried to raise myself up to see.

Just then, without warning, Lynn yelled, "Cut!"

The pilot obediently throttled back, and the plane mushed as it slowed. Then, Lynn dove out the door — alone.

That wasn't the plan. We were supposed to go out together.

The stall warning sounded. Jolly muttered something and waved at me to follow, as he too dove out.

I felt like a sprinter still crouched on his heels after the sound of the gun. I squirmed out from behind the pilot, heaved myself forward into a standing crouch, duck-waddled a few steps to the door, and toppled out into the night.

When my body left the slipstream, I caught sight of the pilot staring down at me, his face lit green by the instrument panel, as he was sucked up into the stars.

I didn't realize I'd forgotten my flashlight until a few seconds after I stabilized in free fall. This oversight now seems impossibly reckless, a foreshadowing of the years I would spend addicted to drugs and alcohol; an omen of future relationships carelessly entered and painfully abandoned; a portent of my episodic life. It steals breath from my narrative, tempts me to quit writing it. But as I continue to recall that night long ago, I find myself less disturbed by my rash, impulsive carelessness and more impressed by the faith that allowed me to hang in there as I fell.

My mind became serenely clear. It was not going to be any other way than this. Time could not be wasted in thinking it might be. There could be no reaching back into the aircraft or looking away from what was happening. Like the time, ten years down the road, when a doctor would tell me that my second child had been born "Mongoloid." Or the night, eighteen months later, after I'd come home from being with him in the hospital, when a nurse would call to say he'd died. Or the night I zipped my father into a body bag. Or the morning I photographed my mother's corpse.

Clarity.

Falling face-to-earth through the night, I was ruled by gravity and time. I had to blink repeatedly to make sure my eyes were open. After a few moments, I could see the shiny steel housing around my altimeter. But the instrument's face remained dark, its phosphorescent needle too dim to read.

I felt the uprushing cushion of air support my body and heard the flapping of my chest strap against the harness. I hadn't fallen for ten seconds before my eyes began to tear beneath my goggles.

Executing a flat right turn, I searched for the target. *Nothing.*

I shook my head, trying to clear the tears, and turned back to the left. *Nothing.* Once, I thought I glimpsed it from the corner of my eye, but then it vanished in the darkness.

The horizon was black, San Diego gone.

When would it seem that dark again? In a sweat lodge on the Pine Ridge Indian Reservation. So dark in there, I will have to shut my eyes. A darkness that will illuminate the black hole of failure: ten thousand bar napkins on which I'd scribbled brilliant insights. The decades spent laboring as a key grip on movies. The years wasted, pretending that I knew how to love. The truth endangered by my fear of it. The laziness. The inspiration pissed away. The countless times I told this very story in bars, giving it away to the wind:

> So, there I am, falling through the night. I could pull the ripcord right now, of course, but then I'd drift for miles over the desert and it'd take them forever to find me, and everyone would think I panicked. *Fuck it,* I tell myself, *keep going.* Then suddenly I remember that Lynn and Jolly are below me. I sure as shit don't want to come crashing through their open canopies at 125 miles per hour, so I go into a tracking mode, like this [I jump off my barstool and assume a delta position, like a ski jumper in midair]: I'm traversing the ground at about 90 miles per hour — which doesn't mean I'm falling any slower — and I keep tracking until I figure there's enough distance between Jolly and Lynn and me, right? Okay, then I relax a little. But I don't like all this blackness — it makes me feel antsy as hell — so I collapse one arm, and I do a half-barrel roll and extend my arm again, like so, and just lie there on my back, looking at the stars. Seeing Orion makes me feel better. Time's gone by, but how much? I flip back over, face down, and tell myself again, *No way in hell I'm going to make an ass of myself by opening high.* But then I start to think, *Shit, if I haven't seen the target yet, I must be way out in the tules, which means they're going to have to come looking for me anyway, so* . . .

By this time, I've kept my audience on the hook way past the time I was supposed to pull the ripcord. I'm standing there on the barroom floor, arms and legs spread as if I were in free fall. A few people are looking at me like I'm already dead. Then I uncork the part they want to hear:

> . . . so, I tell myself, *It's better to be seen as a coward than to cream in without a word.* And I reach across my chest, take hold of the ripcord handle, and pull.

Even now, I can feel the sleeved parachute peeling off my back, and the nylon suspension lines ripping free of the rubber stows. I tense my shoulders, bracing for the opening shock. When it comes, I grip the harness, anticipating the second and final opening.

And then, just as the chute breathes fully open, my feet gently touch the ground, and I find myself standing next to a ball of tumbleweed.

The chute collapses onto the desert floor. I stare ahead into the night.

# 10

# No Feeling of Falling

F ROM MY CURRENT PERSPECTIVE as a college professor, it startles me to remember that in the autumn of
1958, after nine weeks of binge drinking, class cutting,
and compulsory ROTC drills, I blew off my first semester of college and took a train back east to live with my parents and two
younger siblings in a small town forty miles north of New York
City. I announced to my family that I had become an existentialist. In what I see now as penance for wasting my father's money,
I refused to reoccupy my upstairs bedroom and chose instead to
camp on a thin straw mat in a corner of the basement. There I
would sit in half-lotus for hours at a time, reading Camus and
Kierkegaard, drinking strong Darjeeling tea, and smoking un-
filtered Chesterfields. My mother, delighted that I was reading
philosophy, encouraged me to read aloud long sections of Sar-
tre's *Being and Nothingness* while she cooked dinner. My father,
on the other hand, seemed to take my new philosophical asser-
tiveness as a threat. When I informed him, for instance, that
free love was the cool new thing, he told me, "It might interest

you to know that your mother and I kicked up our heels a time or two before you were born."

*Yeah, right,* I thought.

My reading had primed me to defy the ticky-tacky, appliance-happy, postwar American zeitgeist. I aspired to and embraced the Beat life — the rebellious, angst-ridden celebration of rootless America — but my father's comfortable living as a commercial artist and my mother's role as artist and homemaker gave me little to rebel against. The nineteenth-century house, decorated with their paintings, lithographs, sculptures, and drawings, exuded an atmosphere of creativity and taste. They owned only one car and hardly any modern appliances. The house had no shower, just two small bathtubs. We almost never watched TV, and dinner table discussions resembled seminars, with subjects ranging from presidential politics (Ike shouldn't have beaten Adlai a second time) to art (photography threatened to replace the canvas) to sports (could anyone ever top that Willie Mays catch?).

This engaged family atmosphere, and my father's seemingly effortless work-at-home lifestyle, created a problem. I needed him to be a weary, briefcase-toting commuter who went to work in a gray flannel suit every day, and because he wasn't, I was forced to respond to his constant presence in a rude and petulant way that betrayed, with its clumsy resentment, an underlying love and admiration. Clearly he was leading an enviable life, but I had no clue how he had arrived at it.

After I dropped out of college, I saw that my hard-won life experience — two high school summers spent mimicking Kerouac by hitchhiking back and forth across the country, holding an assortment of odd jobs, hopping freight trains, and getting jailed for vagrancy — had no value on an adult résumé. I was supposed to get a real job now, but the jobs available to high school graduates did not square with my romanticized self-image. How could a Beat existentialist stoop to working as a clerk at Macy's? I needed a guide to the real world, but my father knew nothing about résumés, personnel agencies, or help-wanted ads. My mother might as well have been living in the nineteenth century. The youngest child of a stock broker, she had never held a full-time job outside the home.

It didn't help that, having been sent away to private school on a scholarship at age fourteen, I knew almost no one in my hometown. My former classmates, most of them from New York City and Boston, had all gone off to college, where, unlike me, they remained. My high school girlfriend lived in the city, only an hour's train ride away, but with my confidence gone, my libido was in hiding. I simply couldn't get off my mat to go see her.

Every night, I assured my parents that the next day I would catch the first train to New York City and ship out to Europe on a freighter, as I had been threatening to do for months. I could count on my mother to respond kindly: "I know you will, dear." But not my father. Though he made few trips into New York himself — and then only to visit the major museums — he pressed me daily to "buckle down and do it."

"I'm going tomorrow, Dad. Take it easy."

"Where have I heard *that* before?" he would ask. "You said the same thing yesterday! And the day before."

"Don't worry, man," I would tell him. "I've scoped it out. I'm going tomorrow."

It got so that I even convinced myself: *tomorrow* I would do it. But every morning, I would wake up with a terrible sinking sensation and go right back to sleep. I developed a persistent headache. One day dragged into the next and a new year rolled around. I couldn't sleep, and I could make no sense of my waking life. I'd been eighteen years old for nine months, legally adult and free, but I couldn't get out of the basement.

• • •

Then, one evening in late January 1959, after I'd been home for three months, my father ventured into the cellar. He seemed more upbeat than usual, or maybe less pained at the sight of me. He wore a sweater and slippers and clenched a lit pipe between his teeth. Approaching my straw mat with the prudence of a lion tamer, he tossed me the most recent issue of *The New Yorker*, folded open to the "Profiles" page.

"This might be an interesting avenue of approach," he said. Without waiting for my response, he returned upstairs to have an evening cocktail with my mother. I stared at the article, titled "No Feeling of Falling." A crudely drawn illustration depicted a broad-shouldered man wearing a football helmet, bubble goggles, and two parachutes — one on his back and a smaller one on his chest.

Grudgingly I read the first two sentences: "Jacques André Istel, a twenty-nine-year-old French-American with a Princeton education and a distinguished family background of banking and international finance, is the nation's leading parachutist. It is scarcely too much to say that Istel *is* the parachute movement in the United States."

I stood up from my mat and went upstairs to sit on the living room sofa, where the light was better for reading. My sister and brother, when they saw me, began laughing and playing chopsticks on the piano, but I hardly noticed their antics. I learned that Jacques Istel lived with his beautiful wife, Claudia, and his business partner, Lew Sanborn, in a secluded twenty-seven-room hilltop mansion in Bedford, New York, a town that just happened to be only four miles down the road. The writer pointed out that despite Istel's family wealth, he had gained real-world experience by hitchhiking, working odd jobs, and getting into trouble. His thirst for adventure had proved nearly inexhaustible, leading him as a youth into all sorts of delinquent and attention-getting behavior. (At age nine, while playing a game he called "bombardier," he broke all 175 panes of glass in his uncle's greenhouse.) He later became a Marine Corps lieutenant in Korea, and in recent years, a combination of rebelliousness and fastidious discipline had propelled him past many obstacles to a position of prominence in the international parachuting world (whatever *that* was).

As I continued to read, my headache went away and I felt unusually alert. The thirteen-page profile alluded to the military aspects of parachuting and to international parachute competition, and it portrayed the United States as fertile ground for this as-yet-unrecognized sport. The profile writer, Robert Lewis Taylor, concluded that Istel "feels that he is exploring a vast and silent new medium, the deep blue well of the sky, and who knows what may come of it?"

I stood up from the sofa, my head suddenly clear, and joined the family for dinner, then asked my father for the keys to the car.

It is characteristic of all propitious relationships that the moment of first contact seems, in retrospect, inevitable. It happens with love, and it happens with apprenticeships.

It was bitter cold that late January night when I drove to the neighboring town of Bedford. My father had described what he felt sure was the entrance to Istel's property — a nondescript and narrow macadam driveway marked by a battered black mailbox — a few miles east of town. I found the driveway with no problem. Icy in spots, it wound, snakelike, up a very steep and heavily wooded hillside and broke out suddenly into a cul-de-sac directly in front of Istel's stone mansion. I parked my father's two-door Chevy between a vintage Bugati racecar, partially covered with a tarpaulin, and a Mercedes 300-SL convertible. A green Volkswagen Bug and a '57 Chevy station wagon were parked in front of the garage.

I killed the headlights and waited for guard dogs to bark, but nothing broke the silent darkness surrounding the mansion. When a first-floor light came on, I stepped out of the car, took one last hit off my cigarette, and blew smoke at the stars. Leaving my ski cap and coat in the car, I walked to the front door.

It opened just as I was poised to knock.

I had expected someone other than Jacques André Istel to come to the door, but there he stood in khaki pants and a white T-shirt, looking just as "simian" as that *New Yorker* profile had described him: jet black hair, hunched shoulders, jaw and neck thrust forward as if he were some great ape about to beat his chest at a challenger. A normal person might have recoiled, but I was no normal person that night. Perhaps that's why I ignored his hostile affect and took a cue from his expression, which seemed both challenging and hopeful, as if he had all along expected someone to show up on his doorstep at just this time of night, though he wasn't yet willing to grant that I was that person.

"What is it you want?" he asked, his French accent stronger than I had imagined.

"I want to make a parachute jump," I said, rubbing my bare hands together.

Istel chuckled. "Hey, Lew!" he called over his shoulder. I looked beyond Istel, into the wide but completely bare foyer — no furniture or art of any kind — and watched Lew walk jauntily toward the door. He had a pleasant face — smooth-browed, soft, and as wholesome as a Midwestern farmer's — and a welcoming smile.

"Look what the cat dragged in," said Istel.

"Yeah," said Lew, "I see!" He held out his hand to me. "Lew Sanborn."

"Dusty," I said, shaking his hand, then belatedly shaking Istel's.

I stood there shivering while Istel launched into a lengthy

description of his plans to open the first sport-parachuting center in the United States. I hadn't expected a sales pitch, but I listened politely. When Istel was finished, both men stood there staring at me, Sanborn apparently amused by my impulsive late-evening visit.

"We're going to open the center in May," said Istel, his lower jaw thrust forward, as if he were trying to retain a mouthful of water even as he spoke.

"Sounds good," I said, "but when can I make a jump? I might not be around in May."

"Are you looking for work?" Istel asked.

"Yeah," said Sanborn, "are you looking for work?"

Unprepared for the question, I stammered that I was just about to ship out on a Scandinavian freighter headed for a port in Europe. "Going to Brooklyn tomorrow," I said. "Probably ship out within the week. Might be gone a year or two. Don't know."

"Really?" said Istel.

"Hey, that's great," said Sanborn. "A year or two!"

They were toying with me, I could tell, but I didn't let on that I knew. I figured it was a test of some kind.

"Yep," I said. "Just about to ship out. So . . . when can I make a parachute jump?"

"How much does that pay — working on a freighter?" asked Sanborn.

I'd heard rumors that apprentice seamen on non-union freighters earned two dollars and fifty cents a day. "Two-fifty a day," I said. "Plus room and board, obviously. Since it's a freighter."

"Obviously," said Istel, looking at Sanborn and nodding.

"Obviously," said Sanborn, nodding at Istel. "Since it's a freighter."

"Okay," said Istel. "Two dollars and fifty cents a day — that's what we'll pay you." He extended his hand to shake on the deal.

I hesitated. Did he think I was that much of a sucker? I could make two-fifty an *hour*, even without a college degree.

"Plus room and board, of course," said Sanborn, holding a finger up to Istel's face, as if he'd suddenly become my agent. "And the jumps are free, remember that."

"Of course," said Istel, his hand still extended. "You won't get rich working for us," he added "but I'll guarantee you that if you work hard and stick with us, you'll make a name for yourself and have a great time doing it."

He had me. We all shook hands again. And with that, they moved aside and invited me in.

Two days later, at the wheel of Istel's green Volkswagen Beetle, I headed north on a mission to tack up parachuting posters in restaurants, ski centers, and college dorms all over New England. Because I had attended boarding school in southern Vermont, I was familiar with most of the ski centers, the roads, and how to negotiate them in winter (no interstates then). My itinerary would take me straight up to Mont Blanc in Quebec, back down through Vermont, with stops at Stowe, Sugarbush, and Killington, and then east into the White Mountains of New Hampshire, where I'd hit Dartmouth College and Tuckerman's Ravine. Istel fronted me cash for expenses and Sanborn loaded the Beetle with two boxes full of bright orange flyers announcing the May opening of the Orange Sport Parachuting Center, in Orange, Massachusetts. The artfully painted posters depicted a single-engine airplane silhouetted against a white sun. Beneath the plane, a spread-eagled skydiver fell into empty space. JUMPED YET? IT'S GREAT! read the boldface copy. It was the most provocative advertisement I'd ever seen, even more challenging than the war bond posters my father had painted during World War II. One of his had depicted three children standing in the shadow of a Nazi swastika. DON'T LET THAT SHADOW

TOUCH THEM, it warned. That dark challenge had been met. Now it was time for a new adventure, a new test of will. And where better to go than up?

Along with the posters, I carried two main parachutes and a chest-mounted reserve chute. I also packed white coveralls, a pair of thick-soled Corcoran boots, a white football helmet, and bubble goggles.

"Anyone asks," Sanborn had said, "just suit up and give them a full-gear demonstration."

I could not imagine giving such a demonstration to a stranger, especially since I had never even been in a small airplane, much less jumped from one. But I could not wait to try on the gear. I spent the first night in Putney, Vermont, at the home of a former teacher. It snowed the next day and took me eight hours to get into Canada. When a snowplow almost buried the car, I pulled off the main highway just a few miles south of Montreal and stopped at a little roadside establishment called L'Auberge something-or-other. The snow banks in the parking lot were ten feet high.

"How much for a single room?" I asked the middle-aged woman at the reception desk.

"*Vous êtes seul?*" she asked.

"What?" I asked.

"You are alone?" she asked again, apparently disgusted by the need to speak English. Heavy bell-shaped earrings stretched her earlobes to the limit; gravity tugged at her fleshy cheeks.

"Yes," I said. "A single room, please."

She looked at me with suspicious mascaraed eyes.

The room rate did not conform to my strict expense budget, but I had no choice. I signed the register and proudly noted my professional affiliation as Parachutes Incorporated, U.S.A. The woman issued me the room key and pointed to an interior hallway just off the lobby.

"No outside entrance?" I asked, illustrating my question with hand gestures.

"*Comment?*" she asked. She smelled of tobacco and talcum powder.

"Never mind," I said.

I unloaded the car and carried everything — parachutes, kit bags, posters — through a set of glass doors, into the motel lobby, and down the long hall to my spacious room. It took me four or five trips, each step monitored by the huffy proprietor. I dumped everything on the bed. After parking the car, I bought a Coke and some peanuts in the lobby and went to my room, eager to be alone with the equipment.

I stripped off my outer garments and stepped into the jump suit, buttoning it up to the neck. Next, I put on and laced up the spit-polished jump boots, the tops of which came to my mid-calves. I pulled heavy rubber bands over the boots and bloused the cuffs of the coveralls, military style. I stood up, two inches taller in cushioned soles, and admired myself in the large mirror above the dresser.

"Not bad," I said out loud.

I took the free-fall parachute from its kit bag and arranged the harness. Then onto my shoulders I heaved it, like a thirty-pound dinner jacket. Sanborn had told me this particular parachute design was an example of the latest technology — something the U.S. Army was just itching to get its hands on. Gone was the old central-release mechanism used in World War II. On this chute, the chest and leg straps each had a foolproof quick-release buckle, and the suspension lines could be jettisoned easily if you were being dragged along the ground in a high wind.

I had rehearsed all this information on the drive north. Now that I was actually suiting up, it began to make sense. Watching myself in the mirror, I tightened the straps, stowing the excess under a special elastic cover provided for that purpose. I clipped the reserve chute to two D-rings on the front of the harness and cinched the whole business tight to my body. I put on the bubble goggles, donned the football helmet, and snapped the chin strap. The smell of dry silk and the linseed stink of canvas made me feel brave.

Completely outfitted, I gazed in the mirror. Captivated by the person I saw standing there, as I had been mesmerized by photographs and paintings of soldiers when I was a boy, I felt like a man about to pass through a turnstile into some mythic world. It would be easy to underestimate the significance of that moment — pass it off as adolescent posturing — but I think it was precisely then that two energies began to interact within me: desire and will. By desire I don't mean a conscious wanting, as in wanting to be free and heroic, but rather an ill-defined longing — like that of Narcissus — for some satisfactory reflection of myself. And by will, I simply mean *intent*. I did not have to decide anything. As I stared at myself in the mirror, longing was transformed miraculously into intent. It didn't matter that I hadn't jumped yet. At that moment, I had no doubt at all that I would. The proof stood right there in front of me. The commitment was already made. A feeling of warmth spread through my solar plexus, as if I had just swallowed hot soup. I was going to shake off the curse of the college dropout — and escape what I perceived at the time to be my father's limited world. Soon I would be testing the rarefied air of the parachutist.

Only a handful of Americans jumped out of airplanes for fun in those days. Air-to-air free-fall photography did not yet exist. *What would it feel like,* I wondered, *falling all alone through space, free and entirely on my own?* "Like lying on a mattress of air," Istel had said, "no feeling of falling at all."

I could only barely imagine free fall, but I had no trouble envisioning the reputation that would result from such an adventure. Shamelessly, I held an interview with the press right then and there in the motel room. I positioned myself in profile to the mirror, so that I could glance occasionally at the handsome fellow in the glass and admire his strawberry blond hair and his intense blue eyes. I began addressing a very pretty female reporter who just happened to pick me for a private interview and who chose, for some inexplicable reason, to sit cross-legged on the end of the bed, pencil in hand, notepad resting on her otherwise bare knee.

"Am I ever scared?" I said, shooting her a cocky grin. "Well, not scared, exactly. But a modicum of apprehension is healthy when you're jumping from a height of twelve thousand feet or so. After all, you're plummeting toward the earth like a rock. At higher altitudes, lack of oxygen complicates the situation . . . Why, yes, actually, I do. I'm glad you ask. I feel it is important that young people have a challenge such as this, but it is not for the faint of heart, as you can imagine . . . Afraid of heights? Me? . . . Do they always send such pretty reporters to cover international championship events like this? . . . Am I free for dinner? You mean tonight? Should we maybe fool around first?"

Just then there came a loud knock on the door. I froze. "Just a minute!" I shouted, ripping off my helmet and bubble goggles. I began frantically loosening the reserve chute tie-downs. But it was too late. The proprietor, using her own key, opened the door. She gasped when she saw me.

"*Je le savais!*" she screamed.

"What?" I said.

"*Vous n'êtes pas seul!*"

"What?"

Her breast heaved and her gullet trembled. "You are not alone! I knew this!"

"What do you mean?" I asked.

"I hear you talking to her! *Je le savais!* Where is she?"

I couldn't decide which was worse, getting caught harboring an unpaid guest or talking to an imaginary woman.

"Who?" I asked.

The proprietor yanked open the closet door, then tore back the shower curtain. She even got down on all fours and peered under the bed.

"I'm alone!" I protested. I started to explain that I was rehearsing for a part in a movie, but she stood up and stomped out before I could finish.

"Really, it's true!" I called after her. "I *am* alone!"

I was not alone, of course. Not really. You can't be self-conscious and alone at the same time. I turned to the mirror again, my heart pounding with shame, my confidence shaken.

Two weeks later, when Istel and Sanborn sent me to live in Orange, Massachusetts, in a rundown farmhouse on the edge of Orange Municipal Airport, I felt as if I'd been assigned to paradise. Already living in the house were Nate Pond and his father, Sebastian "Batch" Pond. Nate, a twenty-seven-year-old Cornell graduate who had recently become a third partner in Parachutes Incorporated, was well on his way to becoming what my father would have called a "rough customer." What struck me right away was the glint in his eye — at once playful and angry — and his restless staccato laugh. His father was both a gentleman farmer and a pilot. As a young man, Batch had flown the mail in Mexico. He liked his vodka and kept cases of it under his bed. Nate didn't seem to have fallen very far from the tree, though he favored beer. I was assigned the smallest room in the farmhouse. When I got out of bed in the morning, my knees touched the wall. But it was better than the basement at home.

In the late 1950s, western Massachusetts was a region in precipitous decline, following the departure of the textile industry after the war. The town of Orange, though nicely situated in the Berkshires, felt unprosperous and dreary. It reminded me of the coal-mining town in *How Green Was My Valley*, the first movie I saw as a child. Aubuchon's Hardware on Main Street was the place to be during the day, and you had a choice of three establishments in the evening: Frank's Bar, which featured pickled eggs and fifteen-cent glasses of draft beer; the smoke-choked Orange Diner, where you could get a pretty good meatloaf dinner for a couple of bucks; or the upscale DiNapoli's Ristorante, where you could dine in candlelit booths, complete with red-checkered tablecloths, and be served by the owner's sultry, olive-skinned daughter.

I'd come to view devastated towns like Orange through rose-colored glasses — oh, glorious, rootless America! Since I'd never had to live for any length of time in such a place, I was free to admire decay and ignore the misery of the working poor and unemployed. Beneath my romantic view of poverty lay a thinly disguised arrogance born of privilege. I had a developer's eye long before I learned to distrust the process of gentrification that has transformed so many American towns and cities; everywhere, broken-down brick buildings, nonfunctioning watermills, and peeling picket fences resonated with potential. It helped, of course, that I was an advance scout for what would become a noisy invasion of skydivers — one followed closely by reporters and filmmakers. I was riding a gust of fresh air that would very soon put the town on the map.

We began building the jump center in February, when Lew Sanborn arrived from Bedford, bringing his expertise in carpentry and construction. We cleared out the large Quonset-style hangar, erected a wall of parachute storage bins, built six long parachute-packing tables, and suspended a parachute canopy simulator from the I-beams. Next to the hangar, we converted a little wooden building into a classroom and installed thirty antique flip-top desks (complete with inkpots), a portable projection screen, and a rolling blackboard. Sometimes, during coffee breaks, I would light a cigarette and scribble in chalk cryptic messages on the blackboard, like *Cogito ergo sum* or *Beware the philosophical implications of the transcendence of the ego.* Nate would snort with contempt. "You asshole! That's why erasers were invented."

We dumped a truckload of sand near the flight line, then smoothed it out and set up a water-filled fifty-gallon drum to serve as a platform for practicing parachute landing falls (PLFs). We designed and constructed a mockup of a Cessna 182, so students could learn the feel of the open door and rehearse aircraft exits.

Istel had leased Orange Municipal Airport from the town of Orange for twenty years, in exchange for building an aircraft hangar, and on the condition that if Russia invaded America, the airport would revert to its intended purpose as a military evacuation facility. Along with three five-thousand-foot runways, the federal government had built a modern administration building, complete with plate-glass windows, Unicom radio, weather indicators, multidirectional loudspeakers, and a large windsock. Not to mention some pretty nice indoor restrooms and a generous reception area. The large parking lot seemed tailored for our arrival, and, just as Istel had envisioned it, high-octane gas was available and would attract the pilots of multi-engine planes, along with wealthier clientele.

By early March, all the planes and vehicles were painted blue and white, and we had stenciled Istel's company logo everywhere. I began bulldozing a drop zone in the overgrown triangle formed by the intersecting runways. In the evenings — every evening except Sunday, when nothing was open — Lew, Nate, Batch, and I would hit one of the eating establishments and then close Frank's Bar. It's hard to imagine, at this remove, how delicious a pickled egg tasted when seasoned with salt and washed down with a glass of flat Pabst Blue Ribbon draft beer. Perhaps it's less hard to imagine why, instead of buckling down to college life, I preferred coming in from the winter wind after a hard day's work and hanging out with grown men who talked about dangerous things.

Every single night, after listening to tales of bravery and foolishness, and after nearly choking with laughter about close calls and fatal jumps, I would ask Lew or Nate, "So, when can I jump?"

"Maybe tomorrow, if it clears up," Nate would say.

Lew reminded me that the air got ten degrees colder for every thousand feet of altitude. "Soon, Dusty, soon."

› For weeks on end, I acted like one of the men, singing stupid military songs, falling backward in unison off barstools, and arm wrestling, but I still couldn't claim to be one of them. I'd been working in Orange for two months, swaggering in front of townspeople, the way I had postured in front of the motel mirror — and answering their questions with the same empty authority I'd displayed for my imaginary reporter in Montreal. Yet I still hadn't jumped. It began to eat at me: what if I chickened out when the time came? Would I freeze like the airborne jumper Lew told me about, whose knuckles had to be pried loose from the door? That guy was screaming like a baby when they tossed his ass out of the plane. Or worse, what if I froze and they didn't even throw me out of the plane, but just brought me back down and said it was okay? Where could I possibly go after *that*? The tension grew until it was nearly unbearable.

Then, one balmy day in late March, while we ripped eight-foot lengths of tempered masonite through a table saw, Lew suddenly killed the power and asked Nate, "What do you think, should we get it over with?"

"If we have to," growled Nate, taking off his leather nail belt and throwing it on the tarmac. "Goddammit! I guess we have to, right?"

"I mean, we might as well," said Lew, looking exasperated.

"Get what over with?" I asked.

"I mean if we don't, he'll be nagging us right up to opening day," said Lew.

"Pain in the fucking ass," said Nate, spitting a long stream of tobacco juice onto the tarmac.

"If we do it now," said Lew, "maybe he'll shut up and we can get some work out of him."

"Fucking college boys," said Nate, as if he'd never been one himself. "Always nagging. Should draft his ass, send him to Fort Bragg. That'd shut him up."

"Shut who up?" I asked, removing my own nail belt. But I knew who, and I could feel a knot tightening in my stomach.

"We'll give him that old beat-up white canopy," said Lew.

Nate grinned. "You mean the one I used when I jumped in Bulgaria? The one that knocked me unconscious when it opened? Good idea!"

"Either that or the one we took off that dead guy — the one who creamed in down at Stormville. You cleaned the blood off it, right?"

"Sure did," said Nate. "Fucking college boy. I'm getting hungry. Let's get this over with."

"Hey," said Lew, "looks like Batch is already warming up the plane! I'll help him take the door off." He winked at me before he walked away.

"Go over there and get up on that oil drum," ordered Nate.

Suddenly, I didn't want to be alone with Nate Pond. I wanted Lew to be my jumpmaster, kindhearted Lew.

"Do I look like I've got all day?" asked Nate. "Come on, goddammit."

I leapt onto the oil drum and stood there.

"Now put your hands up over your head, like you're holding the parachute suspension lines," said Nate. "Good. Now jump off sideways and do a PLF."

I leapt sideways into the air and landed with my feet together in the sand. The momentum caused me to fall onto my left side, and it carried my feet over my head so that I ended up lying on my right. This absorbed the energy of the fall; I'd been practicing it for months.

"Good," said Nate. "You're ready."

"That's it?" I asked.

"More than I got before my first jump. Fucking Istel. All this pansy-ass training. Come on, get suited up. You already know all this shit."

Ten minutes later, I was sitting on the floor of the Cessna, with my back to the instrument panel, watching Batch adjust the trim tabs after takeoff. I could hardly believe it was finally happening. When I think about it now, from the perspective of a man even older than Batch was back then — when I put myself in the pilot's seat and look down at the kid that was me sitting in the open door — I see a boy struggling with second thoughts. I knew already how to be brave — well, I knew the face of bravery, the affect required — but I also knew too much about the messy consequences of a parachute malfunction. I'd heard a lot of scary jump stories at Frank's Bar. As I gazed down at the sparkling springtime landscape, where newly melted snow was beginning to pool around yellowing willows, the notorious paratrooper song written to the tune of "Beautiful Dreamer" riffed in my head: "Beautiful streamer, open for me. / Blue skies above me but no canopy."

Just before takeoff, Nate had attached my static line to an overhead cable. As we ascended in a widening spiral above the airport, he double-checked the seating of the ripcord pins on my reserve chute. I experienced a surge of apprehension as I watched his cheeks jiggling in the cold air. My stomach felt suddenly bottomless. We made our first pass over the target at twenty-two hundred feet. Nate determined that because of high winds aloft, my exit point would be more than a mile distant from the drop zone, greatly reducing my chances of hearing instructions from Lew, who was waiting down there to guide me to an accurate landing. We soon climbed to twenty-five hundred feet. Batch banked the plane steeply before leveling out on jump run, and again I felt the bottom drop out of my belly. Apprehension threatened to mushroom into fear, but when I took a deep breath, it subsided. As we passed over the target a second time, I swung my legs out into the wind, positioned myself in the doorway, and looked straight down. I saw Lew, half a mile below, staring up at us, his eyes shaded with his right hand, a bullhorn at the ready in his left.

The plane droned on until all the familiar landmarks passed and bare forest was all that was visible below. After shouting a few last-minute course corrections to Batch, Nate put his hand on my shoulder and yelled that I should reach out and grab the wing strut with both hands. He hollered, "Cut!" Batch throttled back, and the plane seemed almost to buck as it slowed to near stall speed. I placed my left foot on a metal step and my right foot on the landing wheel, and I pulled myself out there in the wind. From my perch beneath the high wing, I glanced over my shoulder at Nate and his father; their mouths were pulled back in identical tight-lipped smiles. Suddenly, it felt perfectly natural that I should kick my feet out behind me and push off with both hands.

It felt right to let go.

With a static line, it takes only three or four seconds before the chute opens. A bright red canopy suddenly blossomed above me, and when I looked down I found myself transfixed by the sight of my own two feet dangling so totally free above the earth. This was me alone up here! Gone was the airplane, gone the obnoxious sound of its engine. Through the ear holes in my football helmet I heard only the flapping of nylon in the breeze.

A full minute passed before Lew's amplified voice broke the silence, warning me to turn into the wind to avoid landing in the woods — a precious minute, during which I simply drifted in a self-amazed ecstasy of accomplishment. It was the most intensely private moment of my life up to that time. *If only Dad could see me now!* I thought. I couldn't wait to get down and call my family.

Fifteen months later, in August 1960, a red-and-yellow biplane landed dead-stick on the tarmac, right in front of the airport administration building. Its engine off, the plane touched down silently, bounced once, and then careened wildly between two parked aircraft before screeching to a stop at the gas pumps. A few dozen spectators who had gathered to watch the parachuting let out a collective gasp, as if they'd just witnessed a stunt at some Sunday air show.

Since I was now running the parachuting operation, it was my job to reprimand the pilot. I'd been standing on the flight line, answering some student jumpers' nagging questions about the wind and when it might die down. I excused myself and walked over to the fueling area. With upturned palms, I gave the pilot my best what-the-hell gesture.

"Sorry about that," he yelled. "I plumb ran outta gas!" Craggy-faced and square-jawed, he was wearing a beat-up leather flying helmet and a faded silk scarf. Lifting his oil-spattered aviator goggles, he flashed an appealing grin, completing the iconic image of the outlaw barnstormer. He looked to be about my father's age, but unlike my father, weather-beaten and rugged. I liked the guy right away. I could tell by the sealed-off front cockpit that the plane, a Stearman, was used for crop spraying. I was not about to hassle a working pilot.

"No problem," I told him.

"Go ahead and top it off," he said.

I gassed up the Stearman, took the pilot's cash, and stood back as he gunned the engine and swung the tail around. At the last minute, I ran over and yelled up to him, "Too bad that front seat's closed off, I'd love to jump out of this beast!"

He eased off on the throttle and hollered back, "Get your chute and climb on. I'll take you up right now."

"Climb on?" I asked.

"Right there on the wing. Just watch you don't put your foot through the fabric."

I ran back to my students and told them I was going up to test the wind conditions. "Hang in for a while," I said, grabbing my gear. A few minutes later the Stearman was roaring along runway three-one, with me lying face down on the lower wing, my arms locked around a diagonal strut. It took nearly the full mile of runway to gather enough speed to clear the trees at the end — my body on the wind-whipped wing had disturbed its natural lift. I had to hang on for a good thirty minutes more before we reached a respectable jump altitude of three thousand feet. My elbows ached and my ribs felt numb from lying on my chest-mounted reserve chute, but when I finally stood up and inched my way forward against the powerful prop blast, I experienced a kind of epiphany — one of those moments it takes a lifetime to digest. Looking down over the leading edge of the bright red wing and seeing the landscape glide beneath me — green New England hills dotted with houses, steeples, and cows — I felt a surge of power so pure and thrilling, so sun-lit and masculine, I would draw upon it for years to come. Everything seemed possible. I had earned the future.

In a month, I would leave Orange to begin my first semester at Columbia University. My father had already written the check. I would rent a tiny room near the campus, and New York City would soon swallow me whole. But I didn't know that yet. Just then, I felt decidedly immortal, and when the pilot made a circular gesture with his gloved hand, suggesting we do a back loop, I gave him a heartfelt thumbs-up and hung on for dear life. The earth below disappeared from my view and the sky and sun revolved in a mad crescendo of full-throttled power accompanied by a G-force that nearly buckled my knees.

When the plane leveled, the pilot smiled and jerked his head toward the tail: *Time to get off my wing*. I didn't want to go, didn't want the flight to end. It all seemed so clear from up there. I had discovered the perfect intersection of willingness and opportunity, hidden in an otherwise misty landscape of luck or fate or whatever you want to call the unknown. I could do anything, if I dared.

I pulled myself closer to the engine cowling and inched my way back along the yellow fuselage, careful to step only on the narrow skid-proof surface. "Thanks!" I yelled to the pilot. Then I simply let go, and the wind swept me from the wing like a speck of dust.

# 11

# The Long Road

I HAD A PRETTY GOOD fastball, even at age ten. My father said it made his mitt hand ache. This pleased me at first, but soon his growing reluctance to catch for me in the afternoons began to feel like a chasm opening between us. I started to suspect that his inability to handle my fastball might actually be an inability to handle me. When my parents began discussing the possibility of summer camp, my suspicions were confirmed.

Our house was located between a pristine reservoir and a four-thousand-acre wildlife preserve called the Pound Ridge Reservation — so named because Lenape Indians had once lived and hunted there. Our town was short on kids my age, and what I was learning from the older boys — how to break windows, tip over outhouses, mar road signs, and steal rowboats — wasn't exactly the kind of education my parents had in mind for their firstborn son. But neither was the alternative: roaming a non-peopled realm of fantasy — striding merrily through the woods like Robin Hood, marshaling armies of toy soldiers in my bedroom, or firing hardballs at the slatted side of my father's studio as he worked all day on book illustrations.

Given the natural resources at my disposal, attending summer camp seemed like an exercise in redundancy, but my father announced one evening that Camp Kitchigamink, in Barnard, Vermont, would be "just the ticket." By which I suspected he meant "the cure."

"Just think," he said, "you'll finally learn how to swim."

A quote from Ralph Waldo Emerson graced the cover of Camp Kitchigamink's fifteen-page brochure: "He who knows what sweets and virtues are in the ground, the waters, the plants, the heavens, and how to come at these enchantments, is the rich and royal man."

What the word *kitchigamink* meant, the brochure didn't say, but the camp emblem, a profile of an Indian chief wearing a feathered headdress, gave the place a reassuring authenticity. Indians were the tutelary spirits of white boys in those days, and their skills — fire making, lean-to building, leather crafts, knife and hatchet throwing, and archery — were taught even during the winter in the school gymnasium. To become a rich and royal man, one first had to be an Indian.

My parents, neither rich nor royal in the typical sense, were stingy with their free time. And from my perspective, my eight-year-old sister and three-year-old brother sponged up all the available parental attention, so when it was announced at supper that I was indeed being sent away to camp, I took the expulsion like a warrior. I got into it.

Central Vermont was a haul in those days. When you went away to camp in 1950, you went *away.* My father, meticulous in all things, made the trek sound like a journey to the Himalayas. Out came the maps, the field compass, the army-issue leggings, the canteens, the lists. On went the name labels, the footlocker stickers, the jacket patches. He tried bravely to pave the way for me, telling me how he'd persevered in high school and college, how he'd met my mother and courted her diligently, how he'd used his experience as a war correspondent to further his artistic career. It wasn't a lie, exactly, but his rendering of the past was cleansed of the anxiety I was already feeling about my future.

It was a setup, of course, and the message was clear: to be a rich and royal man meant being an achiever. Success required setting and meeting goals. Awards and kudos, while certainly not everything, were of necessity the mark of the man. With all this firmly in mind, I waved goodbye to my family and rode to Vermont with the head counselor, Mr. Noyes, in his beat-up station wagon.

Camp Kitchigamink consisted of seven tiny cabins clustered on a grassy hillside south of Silver Lake. Slapped together with pine logs and rough-hewn cedar planks, each cabin contained five double bunks — precarious, squeaky structures bedecked with thin, mildewed mattresses crawling with bugs. Every other night some kid woke up screaming with a tick on his eyelid or scrotum.

My first night there, I cried soundlessly into my pillow until I fell asleep. When I woke up, I was in love with the place. Populated with boys ranging in age from eight to fifteen, it sounded, when you closed your eyes, like a forest teeming with birds. Yet it was run like a boot camp. Every boy was on the same page: buddy systems in the lake, jousting competitions on the grass, obstacle courses in the woods, play acting in the outdoor amphitheater, roaring campfires with drumming and whooping and loincloths and headdresses. The air vibrated from dawn to dusk with the shrill sound of whistles. The daily pulse of victory and defeat, ruled as it was by the overarching principle of survival in the adult world, sustained us as we could never have been sustained at home.

So, I learned to swim — and to keep my eye on the prize.

There were four prizes, kept behind glass in the counselors' office until the awards ceremony at the end of the summer. Four gold cups resembling those double-handled trophies you see race-car drivers and hockey players hoisting aloft and kissing. But considerably smaller — twelve inches high and weighing a pound, if that. *Yellowish* might be a more accurate word for the cups, but they shone like gold to me. I studied those trophies whenever I got a chance, memorizing the categories for which they would be given: Greatest Improvement, Greatest Leadership, Greatest Achievement, and (ta-da!) Camper of the Year.

As if underscoring how far behind I'd been when I first arrived at camp, my name was called for the first category during the final campfire ceremony in August. On returning home, I greeted my father with the Greatest Improvement cup held victoriously over my head.

"Hey, Dad, look!"

His reaction was less ecstatic than I'd expected. "Just remember," he warned, "trophies aren't everything."

Still, I placed the cup on my bedroom mantelpiece, alongside a Hopi pottery bowl. That night, I fell asleep staring at its glowing shape in the dark.

The second summer, 1951, I arrived at camp armed with confidence. On June 30, I wrote home: "Dear Folks, Did you get my second letter but if you didn't the important points were more money." Being exactly that pushy, I walked away in August with the Greatest Leadership cup. At home, my siblings were dutifully impressed, but my father seemed to hardly notice my victory. When I placed the cup in the center of the dinner table, he paused significantly in his carving of the roast. My mother asked me to put the cup on the floor.

"Be a little less full of yourself, I think," she said. "Tone down the volume a touch."

But for me, things were falling into place. I was eleven years old, and I had the sense that I was, in some mysterious fashion, *on my way.* That autumn, two boys my age moved to our town. Hungry for company and eager for troops to lead, I organized a camping trip in the reservation behind our house — a survival test, I dubbed it. My new recruits brought along air mattresses, pillows, and comic books. I made a mental note never to invite them again. It was to be a long winter.

When I turned twelve, my father agreed to one more year of camp. Then, he warned, it would be time to think of "other things." I knew he meant a summer job. This presented a problem. There were four cups to win, but I was only going to have three years of camp. Like the Oscar for Best Picture, the presentation of the cup for Camper of the Year was always saved for last and was thus the most coveted. I simply had to have it before moving on to "other things."

So, in the summer of 1952, I hit the ground running. It seemed there was nothing I couldn't do. Not only did I get my intermediate swimmer's patch, but my name was burned into the wooden roster of Sons of Neptune, after I crawled and backstroked and butterflied the entire length of Silver Lake, behind Mr. Noyes's aluminum rowboat.

I pitched a night game under the lights in Lebanon, New Hampshire, climbed Mount Washington faster than anyone else, paddled the White River and the Connecticut. No one could start a fire with flint and steel faster than me. No one was more eager to help Dick Merck — the savvy counselor from Chicago. I followed his lead obediently, led others when called to, and paced myself until the very last day. Looking over my shoulder, as I approached the finish line, I saw no competitors at all.

That last afternoon of camp is as vivid to me now as if I'd been beamed back in time. I'm walking with Dick Merck, up the grassy, clover-strewn hillside between the cabins and the lake. The low sun casts long shadows from the nearby woods, bringing a welcome coolness to my bare feet. Dick and I have just stowed the canoes and life preservers. Battened down the hatches, as my father would have said. Only dinnertime — during which the counselors will vote in private — stands between this moment and the very end of the campfire ceremony, when Mr. Noyes will surely name me Camper of the Year.

Veering off toward his cabin, Dick says, "See you tonight, Dusty."

I need only answer, "See ya." Nothing else is called for. To campaign openly for myself this close to the polls would only guarantee defeat. But as I watch Dick move away, a dark uncertainty envelops me. I must know how this is going to end — ensure the ending — right now.

I've since heard it said that the Zuni Indians of New Mexico call living into old age "the long road." They also use that phrase to identify the life path of certain youngsters they deem difficult — those who don't trust that life must be lived logically from the beginning, through a middle, to the end, and who are lost in an A-to-Z world. Those who refuse to be taught. Those who break the rules, push the limits, test the boundaries, and take forbidden risks. The squirmers, the gazers, the contrarians. For these children, the path ahead is never straight or predictable or safe, but always twisty and uncertain and dangerous. At the end of the path might lie insight and wisdom — maybe even medicine — but surviving to reach that end, there's the trick.

"Hey, Dick," I call out.

He stops. Do I read a warning in the reluctant way he turns to look at me? Is there some way, still, to take back the words that already have begun to issue from my mouth like bees from a hive? As the earth drops out between my father's path and mine, do I perceive — if only for an instant — the nearly endless road ahead?

"Don't forget to vote for me tonight!" I yell, before I can stop myself. My voice hangs in the still air, quieting even the birds, then falls in among the silent shadows.

# 12

# The Second Person

Thy firmness makes my circle just,
And makes me end where I begun.
— JOHN DONNE, "A Valediction
Forbidding Mourning"

IT BEGAN WHEN your mother sent you off to kindergarten with an oval-shaped, pink-and-white-checked lunch box. This during World War II, when most schoolboys carried black lunch pails with coved thermos compartments or just brown-bagged it. Your father was in Normandy at the time, your mother simply exercising her feminine prerogative. And, to be fair, you hadn't objected; you'd kind of liked the oval shape. If the pink part gave you pause, you can't remember now. Cap guns and lassos were your thing. A lunch box was a lunch box. Or so you thought. Until the hooting of your fellow kindergartners set a humiliation threshold that would inform you for years to come. You "lost" the lunch box during recess.

But it started you wondering about yourself, didn't it? Not about your sexual identity or anything like that, but about your headlong, instinctual self and how that self was going to be received in the world. This wondering — the beginnings of caution, perhaps — was new. Life until then had been a consistent breeze. Like the time you were being strollered along a sidewalk near your house in Cambridge, Massachusetts. You reached out and grabbed a chocolate ice cream cone from the hand of an unsuspecting child being strollered in the opposite direction. "The whole scoop went right into your mouth," your mother told you, years later, "and you thought nothing of it, even when the child's mother protested." And you know it's true, don't you? Even now, it's only the habit of civility that keeps your appetites in check.

Predictably enough, right after the lunch box incident, you stole another boy's cap gun. Without a qualm, you jammed the pistol barrel into your belt, concealed the butt with your jacket, and brought the weapon back to your house. You stood in the window of your second-story bedroom, practicing your aim and picking off pedestrians. When you saw the boy's mother march her son toward your house, you panicked. You opened the window and tossed the gun out, hoping they'd find it on the grass and leave you alone. But the gun landed on the sidewalk — which is how, as your mother was spanking you with a hairbrush, you learned the word *smithereens*.

You began life as a thief, and a bold one. But there was something in the world — the world of your family and your kind, at least — that did not embrace the thief. And something in you that couldn't quite stomach public disapproval. You learned to modify your behavior and negotiate desire. You couldn't wait to grow up.

You're sixteen; you've found the Beats. Ecstasy (the mindset, not the drug) is your thing. This summer, you've been imbibing cheap Chianti, rolling Bull Durham cigarettes, reciting Kerouac.

You've dreamt of traversing "the holy void of uncreated empti-
ness." You've longed for a glimpse of "the magic mothswarm of
heaven," and you're now prepared to take "the complete step
across chronological time into timeless shadows."

The complete step seems to involve a tolerable amount of
lawlessness — anything from simple car theft to hitchhiking
across America. Unfamiliar with the techniques of hot-wir-
ing a car, you've chosen the latter, and right now you're standing on the outskirts of Brattleboro, Vermont, with your thumb
stuck out. A state police cruiser passes in the opposite direction. It will be ten years before you call a cop a *pig*, but something about the way this trooper looks at you makes your skin
crawl. A Spanish couple with a baby stops and picks you up.
You jump into the back seat of their Chevy. They're going all
the way to New York City. For about a mile you babble at them
in your best prep-school Spanish. You coo-coo the baby. Then,
suddenly, the police cruiser is alongside you, forcing the couple's car off the road. Before you know it, you're being dragged
out, thrown over the trunk, frisked, kicked in the balls, thrown
into the back of the cruiser, and accused of car theft. You deny
it. You don't know *how* to steal a car, you protest; you've never
even *been* in Rhode Island, where the theft is said to have taken
place. As you're being pummeled, word comes over the police
radio that the real thief (your double, it seems) has been seen
entering a house in another part of town. You're thrown out of
the cruiser, your black carry bag heaved out after you. Later, in
Springfield, Massachusetts, you'll get nabbed again for the same
car theft and released again without apology. It will prove mildly
disappointing not to be jailed, but the blessing of being freed
isn't lost on you, is it? You know something of what it feels like
to be an outlaw now, without having to pay the price. You relish
the story.

•  •  •

You're twenty-four years old and testing the yarmulke atop your head. The bobby pins keep slipping. You glance at your boss, a candidate for the U.S. Senate, before entering the Brooklyn synagogue. He's wearing his yarmulke too, and you want to laugh because it looks as out of place on him as it does on you. You admire this man — so much that you've adopted his accent (*come hee-ah, go they-ah*). As his advance man, it's your job to pass him a couple of index cards with the names of the rabbis and politicians he must acknowledge before his speech. You precede him into the large hall, signaling him to follow. A burst of applause accompanies not his but your entrance — just for a second — until people realize that, although you are handsome and ruddy-complected and wearing a pinstripe suit, you aren't Bobby Kennedy. This will happen often during the Senate campaign, in hotel hallways and motorcades — just a flicker of confusion, enough to let you know what it would be like to be recognized and greeted with such sustained adulation. Enough to give you a hint, but only a hint, of what it must have felt like to walk into that kitchen in Los Angeles and be shot in the head by a stranger.

You're thirty-two. Fidel Castro's a declared enemy of America, Vietnam's raging on, the Kennedys are dead, and you're in the Dominican Republic trying to get a divorce. There's a rumor that last night, nine of Castro's men sneaked ashore in a rubber life raft, and three of them have already been caught and killed. This rumor should be of more than passing interest to you. When you were fifteen, you and your buddies plotted to run away from your Vermont prep school and join Castro's revolution in Cuba. But if today's rumor has made any impression on you, it's a hazy one. You have a hangover; your new girlfriend is waiting impatiently in the hotel; you want to get the legal business over with, so you can have sex in the waters off Boca Chica.

You and your Dominican divorce lawyer — your *abogado* — are stuck in a taxi at a roadblock. A young Dominican soldier, carrying a rifle, demands your passport. You hand it to him. The soldier examines your out-of-date photo. He looks at you quizzically, trying to reconcile your hippie hairdo with the close-cropped sideburns in the photo, your meditation beads with the necktie, your wild Indian headband with the college boy's brow he sees before him in black and white. In no time, he's got the muzzle of his M1 up against your right temple. He seems to be rehearsing the word *freeze*. You glance at your *abogado*, who's gone pale. The soldier orders you into the front seat, gets in behind you, and jams the gun up against the occipital region of your brain. You're driven along bumpy streets to the nearest fort — a two-story building, surrounded by colorful plantings — and, once inside, escorted up a wide wooden staircase. A large oak door is thrown open and you see a puffy-chested army captain sitting at his desk at the far end of an otherwise empty room. The young soldier forces you to your knees, keeping the rifle at the back of your head. "*Aqui esta otro Cubano!*" he says proudly. A look of incredulity comes over the captain's face; a huge grin appears beneath his thick mustache; you're sure he's about to order your execution. Instead, he stands up and moves out from behind his desk, revealing his side arm. He slaps both knees. "*Cubano!?*" he howls. "*Cubano!?*" He strides toward you, choking with laughter, tears streaming from his eyes. He orders the soldier from the room, shakes your hand, apologizes in English. That afternoon, divorced and standing tall with your girlfriend wrapped around you in the salty waters off Boca Chica, you know, at last, something of what it feels like to be a Cuban revolutionary.

What is this pseudo life? Have you ever owned up to being the imposter that you are? If you died right now, wouldn't a reader glean from your scribbled journals that you are capable of imagining almost any life but your own? Wouldn't it come to light that you've been content with success by association? That mere brushes with fame seem to stand in for the real thing? What kind of lunch box are you? Will you now admit that there have been times when you've let people assume you're a stunt man, which they sometimes do when they see you wearing a Stunt Specialist cap? Would it be unbearable to confess that in spite of your high-minded stance against the Vietnam War, you wouldn't mind at all if people thought you'd been a Green Beret back then — a possibility suggested by the fact that you're wearing one now?

Go on, say it, get it all out. When Annie Leibovitz, the famous photographer, came rushing up to you on a film set, where you were employed as a key grip, and gushed about the last time she'd worked with you and how much your work in film has meant to her, you let her go on and on, even though you knew she'd confused you with someone who actually *was* talented and famous. Why? How could you have enjoyed the rub of recognition, or even write about it now, if you'd done nothing to earn it? Who *are* you? To what end, and for what purpose, have you lived this preposterous, imposterish life?

How about the time, a few years back, when you quit working on movies and took a fellowship at a writer's colony? Remember? One night at dinner, a successful poet leaned toward you and asked in a whisper, "Are you somebody famous and I don't know it?" Remember your enigmatic smile? What else did you have to offer her?

Well, here you sit, in your sixties, on a bench in New York City's Riverside Park, your usual indignation about global warming muted for the moment by pleasant late-November sunshine. Green leaves still cling to certain stubborn trees. You can identify with that. It's midday; most people are at work. You sit here like some ridiculous census taker, laptop on your knees, gazing at passersby, trying to create something significant out of nothing. The traffic on the West Side Highway hisses and thrums like surf. A Jamaican nanny is wheeling a stroller your way. A blond, blue-eyed child is seated in it. As the stroller passes your bench, the child spies you fingering the keys of your laptop. He wrenches around in his seat, locks his eyes on yours, and smiles. For an instant — and an instant is all you need — you know what you are going to be when you grow up.

# Acknowledgments

My heartfelt thanks to Columbia University staff and faculty, whose guidance sustained me while I completed my MFA at age sixtysomething: John Bowers, Nicholas Christopher, Lis Harris, Colette Inez, Michael Janeway, Raymond Kennedy, Richard Locke, Honor Moore, Patricia O'Toole, Anna Delmoro Peterson, Phyllis Raphael, Michael Scammell, Mark Slouka, Nancy Worman, and Alan Ziegler.

I am grateful to the following people for seeing merit in my work and shepherding it into print: Don Erickson and Edward Klein (*New York Times Magazine*); Mark Drew, Peter Stitt, and Mindy Wilson (*Gettysburg Review*); Leslie T. Sharpe (*Quarto*); Karen Mann and Sena Jeter Naslund (*Louisville Review*); Joe Mackall and Terence Smyre (*River Teeth*, University of Nebraska Press); Joan Connor and Catherine Taylor (*Hotel Amerika*); Ronald Spatz (*Alaska Quarterly Review*); and Nicole Angeloro, Susanna Brougham, and Deanne Urmy (Houghton Mifflin).

Without the support of family, friends, and colleagues, writing is impossible. I thank my daughter, Trellan Karr Smith, and her mother, Catherine Smith; my sister, Leslie Borden; my brother, Lochlin Smith; my ex-wife Lucille Masone Smith; and my adopted brother, Mike Little Boy, and his family. My friends from skydiving days — Jim Arender, Steve Boyle, Jacques

Istel, Walt Penn, Larry and Gloria Pond, Nate and Jill Pond, and Lewis B. Sanborn — still keep me safe and sane though I no longer jump out of planes. I am forever in debt to all those folks in the film industry for providing me with memorable stories; though I cannot name them all here, I would be remiss if I did not thank Bob Andres, Haddon Hufford, Gary Martone, and Rex North for making me laugh and watching my back. My friends — those who critiqued various versions of these essays or read my work as it appeared in print or simply inspired me — include Mary Weasel Bear, Rachel Bell, Marcia F. Brown, Nat Clifford, Sam Furth, Scott Hillier, Nancy Lord, Peg MacLeish, Suzanne Menghraj, Forrest Murray, Carol Paik, Angela Patrinos, Jack Ryan, Mimi Schwartz, Penelope Schwartz-Robinson, Peter Selgin, Joyin Shi, Jim Sprouse, and David and Sarah Stromeyer.

I have the good fortune to thank Terry Tempest Williams, who selected my manuscript for the Katharine Bakeless Nason Prize in Creative Nonfiction, and Michael Collier and Ian Pounds from the Breadloaf Writers' Conference at Middlebury College, which sponsors the prize.

Most especially, I want to thank Kim Dana Kupperman, without whose faith, love, and selfless collaboration this volume would not exist.

# Bread Loaf and the Bakeless Prizes

The Katharine Bakeless Nason Literary Publication Prizes were established in 1995 to expand the Bread Loaf Writers' Conference's commitment to the support of emerging writers. Endowed by the LZ Francis Foundation, the prizes commemorate Middlebury College patron Katharine Bakeless Nason and launch the publication career of a poet, a fiction writer, and a creative nonfiction writer annually. Winning manuscripts are chosen in an open national competition by a distinguished judge in each genre. Winners are published by Houghton Mifflin Company in Mariner paperback original.

2007 JUDGES

Stanley Plumly, *poetry*

Amy Hempel, *fiction*

Terry Tempest Williams, *creative nonfiction*